quick and easy meals

vegetarian

Styling and Food DONNA HAY
Photography WILLIAM MEPPEM

TRIDENT
PRESS
INTERNATIONAL

Introduction

Some like it hot! That's the simple premise for this collection of fresh, new vegetarian food ideas.

The recipes are judiciously seasoned with chillies, fresh ginger, mustard, cumin and peppercorns (among others), to make the diner's taste buds stand up and take notice of a healthy, meatless way of eating that is delightfully exciting.

This book is packed with taste sensations from around the world and will appeal to anyone looking for great food with a spicy kick.

Published by:
TRIDENT PRESS INTERNATIONAL
801 12th Avenue South
Suite 302
Naples, FL 34102 U.S.A.
(c)Trident Press
Tel: (941) 649 7077
Fax: (941) 649 5832
Email: tridentpress@worldnet.att.net
Website: www.trident-international.com

Quick & Easy Meals for the Vegetarian

Production Director: Anna Maguire
Recipe Development: Judy Vassallo
Food Photography: William Meppem
Food Styling: Donna Hay
Food Stylist's Assistant: Stephanie Elias

Includes Index
ISBN 1 58279 095 7
EAN 9 781582 790954

First Edition Printed May 2001
Printed by Toppan Printing, Hong Kong

ABOUT THIS BOOK

INGREDIENTS

Unless otherwise stated the following ingredients are used in this book:

Cream — Double, suitable for whipping
Flour — White flour, plain or standard
Sugar — White sugar

CANNED FOODS

Can sizes vary between countries and manufacturers. You may find the quantities in this book are slightly different to what is available. Purchase and use the can size nearest to the suggested size in the recipe.

MICROWAVE IT

Where microwave instructions occur in this book, a microwave oven with an output power of 850 watts (IEC705 – 1988) or 750 watts (AS2895 – 1986) was used. The output power of most domestic microwaves ranges between 600 and 900 watts (IEC705 – 1988) or 500 and 800 watts (AS2895 – 1986), so it may be necessary to vary cooking times slightly depending on the output power of your microwave.

WHAT'S IN A TABLESPOON?

AUSTRALIA
1 tablespoon = 20 mL or 4 teaspoons
NEW ZEALAND
1 tablespoon = 15 mL or 3 teaspoons
UNITED KINGDOM
1 tablespoon = 15 mL or 3 teaspoons
The recipes in this book were tested in Australia where a 20 mL tablespoon is standard. The tablespoon in the New Zealand and the United Kingdom sets of measuring spoons is 15 mL. For recipes using baking powder, gelatine, bicarbonate of soda, small quantities of flour and cornflour, simply add another teaspoon for each tablespoon specified.

Contents

Light 'n' Easy

RED LENTIL FELAFEL WITH DIP

500 g/1 lb red lentils
2 cups/125 g/4 oz breadcrumbs, made
from stale bread
1 onion, chopped
4 dried red chillies, crushed
4 tablespoons chopped fresh parsley
1 clove garlic, crushed
2 teaspoons ground cumin
2 eggs
vegetable oil for deep-frying

MINTY YOGURT DIP
2 tablespoons shredded fresh mint
1 teaspoon ground cumin
$^1/_2$ teaspoon chilli powder
1 cup/200 g/6$^1/_2$ oz natural yogurt
2 tablespoons lemon juice

1   Place lentils and 4 cups/1 litre/1$^3/_4$ pt
water in a saucepan and bring to the
boil over a medium heat. Reduce heat
and simmer, stirring occasionally, for
15-20 minutes or until lentils are tender
and liquid is absorbed – there should be
about 4 cups/1 litre/1$^3/_4$ pt cooked
lentils. Set aside to cool.

2   Place lentils, breadcrumbs, onion,
chillies, parsley, garlic, cumin and eggs
in a food processor and process until a
soft ball forms. Take 2 tablespoons of
mixture and shape into flat balls.

3   Heat oil in a large saucepan until a
cube of bread dropped in browns in
50 seconds then deep-fry felafel, a few
at a time, for 4 minutes or until brown.
Drain on absorbent kitchen paper.

4   To make dip, place mint, cumin,
chilli powder, yogurt and lemon juice
in a bowl and mix to combine. Serve
with felafel.

Makes 24

For a light meal, place felafel
on flat bread top with
shredded lettuce, chopped
tomatoes and finely sliced
onions, then drizzle with the
dip and roll up.

MIDDLE EASTERN GARLIC DIP

Oven temperature
200°C, 400°F, Gas 6

3 medium eggplant (aubergines),
cut into 1 cm/$^1/_2$ in thick slices
salt
4 cloves garlic, unpeeled
$^1/_2$ cup/125 mL/4 fl oz olive oil
1 tablespoon paprika
1 tablespoon ground cumin
1 teaspoon sugar
$^1/_2$ teaspoon harissa
$^1/_2$ cup/125 mL/4 fl oz water
2 tablespoons chopped fresh mint
$^1/_4$ cup/60 mL/2 fl oz lime juice

1   Place eggplant (aubergines) in a
colander, sprinkle with salt and set
aside for 30 minutes. Rinse under cold
water and pat dry with absorbent
kitchen paper.

2   Place eggplant (aubergine) slices
and garlic in a baking dish and brush
with oil. Bake for 20 minutes or until
eggplant (aubergines) and garlic are
golden and very tender.

3   Peel garlic cloves. Place eggplant
(aubergines), garlic, paprika, cumin,
sugar and harissa in a bowl and mash
lightly to make a rough paste.

4   Place eggplant (aubergine) mixture
in a nonstick frying pan, add water
and cook, stirring, over a medium heat
for 10 minutes or until the liquid is
absorbed. Remove pan from heat and
stir in mint and lime juice.

Serves 6

Serve with crusty Italian-style
or wood-fired bread, pitta
crisps or fresh vegetables
for dipping.
Harissa is a very hot chilli
paste, for more information
and a simple homemade
version see hint on page 30.

CHILLI POLENTA WITH CHEESE

5 cups/1.2 litres/2 pt water
1³/4 cups/300 g/9¹/2 oz corn meal
(polenta)
1 tablespoon chilli paste (sambal oelek)
2 tablespoons grated Parmesan cheese
30 g/1 oz butter

CHEESE AND NUT TOPPING
125 g/4 oz hazelnuts, roasted and
chopped
90 g/3 oz ricotta cheese, drained
90 g/3 oz goat's cheese, crumbled
45 g/1¹/2 oz butter, softened
2 tablespoons snipped fresh chives
1 tablespoon wholegrain mustard

1   Place water in a large saucepan and bring to the boil. Reduce heat to simmering, then gradually whisk in corn meal (polenta) and cook, stirring, for 20 minutes or until mixture is thick and leaves the sides of the pan.

2   Remove pan from heat and stir in chilli paste (sambal oelek), Parmesan cheese and butter. Spread mixture evenly into a lightly greased 23 cm/9 in square cake tin and refrigerate until set.

3   To make topping, place hazelnuts, ricotta and goat's cheeses, butter, chives and mustard in a bowl and mix to combine.

4   Cut set polenta into diamonds and place on a nonstick baking tray. Cook under a preheated hot grill for 2 minutes or until golden. Turn polenta over, top each diamond with 1 tablespoon topping and grill for 1-2 minutes longer or until golden.

Serves 4

Corn meal (polenta) is cooked yellow maize flour and is very popular in northern Italian cooking. Polenta refers to both the name of the dish and the yellow maize flour.

Chilli Polenta with Cheese

Blue bowl Freedom

BLACK-EYED BEAN NACHOS

250 g/8 oz black-eyed beans, soaked
for 2-5 hours and drained
2 teaspoons vegetable oil
2 onions, chopped
4 dried red chillies, crushed
1 tablespoon cumin seeds
2 x 440 g/14 oz canned tomatoes,
undrained and chopped
1/2 cup/125 mL/4 fl oz red wine
2 tablespoons tomato paste (purée)
2 teaspoons sugar
3 tablespoons chopped fresh coriander
250 g/8 oz corn chips
60 g/2 oz grated tasty cheese (mature
Cheddar)
1 avocado, chopped
2 tablespoons lime juice
sour cream
chilli sauce

Black-eyed beans are also
known as cowpeas, black-
eyed peas and China peas.
They are a white kidney-
shaped bean with a black
eye. As they are a soft
bean they do not have to
be soaked for as long as
and cook more quickly
than other beans such as
red kidney and lima.

1 Place beans in a saucepan and pour
over fresh cold water to cover beans by
about 5 cm/2 in. Bring to the boil and

boil for 10 minutes. Reduce heat, cover
and simmer for 35 minutes or until beans
are tender. Drain well and set aside.

2 Heat oil in a frying pan over a
medium heat, add onions, chillies
and cumin seeds and cook, stirring, for
3 minutes or until onion is soft. Add
tomatoes, wine, tomato paste (purée),
sugar and beans and simmer for
10 minutes or until mixture reduces
and thickens. Stir in coriander.

3 To serve, place corn chips on a
heatproof serving plate and sprinkle
with cheese. Cook under a preheated
grill for 2 minutes or until cheese melts.
Scatter with avocado and sprinkle lime
juice, then spoon over bean mixture and
serve with sour cream and chilli sauce.

Serves 4

BUTTER BEAN DIP

375 g/12 oz dried lima (butter) beans,
soaked overnight and drained
2 bay leaves
6 sprigs fresh thyme or lemon thyme
4 cloves garlic, crushed
2 spring onions, chopped
1 tablespoon chopped fresh
lemon thyme
1 tablespoon chopped fresh parsley
2 teaspoons ground cumin
olive oil
1/4 cup/45 g/1 1/2 oz natural yogurt
2 tablespoons lemon juice
freshly ground black pepper
2 teaspoons paprika

Delicious served with char-
grilled vegetables and your
favourite crusty bread for
dipping.
If lemon thyme is
unavailable use ordinary
thyme and a little finely
grated lemon rind.

1 Place beans in a saucepan, add bay
leaves and thyme sprigs and pour over
fresh cold water to cover beans by about

5 cm/2 in. Bring to the boil and boil for
10 minutes. Reduce heat and simmer
for 1 hour or until beans are very tender.

2 Drain beans and reserve 1/4 cup/
60 mL/2 fl oz of the cooking liquid.
Discard bay leaves and thyme.

3 Place beans, garlic, spring onions,
chopped thyme, parsley, cumin, 1/2 cup/
125 mL/4 fl oz oil and reserved cooking
liquid in a food processor or blender
and process until smooth. Add yogurt,
lemon juice and black pepper to taste
and mix to combine. Spoon into a
bowl, then drizzle with a little olive oil
and sprinkle with paprika.

Serves 6

PASTA WITH ROCKET AND CHILLI

Black pepper fettuccine and chilli oil are available from gourmet delicatessens and some supermarkets. If black pepper fettuccine is unavailable this dish is just as delicious made with ordinary pasta. You can find a recipe for making chilli oil on page 74.

500 g/1 lb black pepper fettuccine
2 tablespoons chilli oil
3 tablespoons lime juice
1 large bunch rocket, leaves shredded
90 g/3 oz grated Parmesan cheese
2 tablespoons fresh basil leaves
freshly ground black pepper

1   Cook pasta in boiling water in a large saucepan following packet directions. Drain well and place in a serving bowl.

2   Add chilli oil and lime juice and toss to combine. Add rocket, Parmesan cheese, basil and black pepper to taste and toss well. Serve immediately.

Serves 6 as a light meal or 4 as a main meal

LEEK AND BASIL FRITTATA

*Above: Leek and Basil Frittata
Opposite: Pasta with Rocket and
Chilli*

5 eggs
$^1/_2$ cup/125 mL/4 fl oz milk
4 tablespoons grated Parmesan cheese
freshly ground black pepper
1 tablespoon olive oil
2 leeks, chopped
125 g/4 oz marinated char-grilled
eggplant (aubergine), cut into strips
3 tablespoons fresh basil leaves

1   Place eggs, milk, Parmesan cheese
and black pepper to taste in a bowl and
whisk to combine. Set aside.

2   Heat oil in a 23 cm/9 in nonstick
frying pan over a medium heat, add
leeks and cook, stirring occasionally,
for 8 minutes or until soft and golden.

3   Stir in eggplant (aubergine) and
basil and cook for 1 minute. Pour egg
mixture over vegetables and cook over
a low heat for 7 minutes or until frittata
is almost set. Place frittata under a
preheated hot grill and cook for 1 minute
or until top is golden and firm. Serve
hot, warm or cold cut into wedges.

Serves 4

Char-grilled marinated
eggplant (aubergine) is
available from gourmet
delicatessens. To make your
own marinated eggplant
(aubergine), marinate
char-grilled eggplant
(aubergine) in olive oil and
lemon juice, seasoned to
taste with freshly ground
black pepper for at least
2 hours. For a spicy kick,
add some finely chopped
red chilli.

VEGETABLE SKEWERS WITH TAHINI

When threading the vegetables onto the skewers make sure that the vegetables have a flat outside surface – this will make them easier to grill. Tahini is a thick oily paste made from crushed toasted sesame seeds. On standing the oil tends to separate out and before using it is necessary to beat it back into the paste. It is available from Middle Eastern food and health food stores and most supermarkets.

3 zucchini (courgettes), cut into
2 cm/^{3}/4 in cubes
2 red peppers, cut into 2 cm/^{3}/4 in cubes
2 yellow or green peppers, cut into
2 cm/^{3}/4 in cubes
8 patty pan squash, halved
185 g/6 oz feta cheese, cut into
2 cm/^{3}/4 in cubes
2 tablespoons chilli oil

TAHINI DIP
^{1}/2 cup/125 g/4 oz tahini
3 tablespoons thick natural yogurt
2 tablespoons lime juice
1 tablespoon sweet chilli sauce
1 tablespoon tomato paste (purée)
freshly ground black pepper

1 Thread zucchini (courgettes), red and yellow or green peppers, squash and feta cheese onto lightly oiled skewers. Brush skewers with oil and cook on a preheated hot barbecue or under a hot grill for 2 minutes each side or until brown and vegetables are tender crisp.

2 To make dip, place tahini, yogurt, lime juice, chilli sauce, tomato paste (purée) and black pepper to taste in a bowl and mix to combine. Serve with kebabs.

Serves 4

TOFU LAVASH WITH SALSA

Lavash bread is a yeast-free bread which is packed in flat sheets. Its history goes back to Biblical times in Syria. It is available from Middle Eastern food shops and some supermarkets.

1 tablespoon finely grated fresh ginger
3 tablespoons soy sauce
2 teaspoons sesame oil
250 g/8 oz firm tofu, cut into
thick strips
4 sheets lavash bread or 4 large pitta
bread rounds
155 g/5 oz baby spinach leaves
3 plum (egg or Italian) tomatoes,
sliced

MANGO SALSA
1 mango, peeled and chopped
2 tablespoons chopped fresh mint
1 fresh red chilli, seeded and chopped
1 tablespoon brown sugar
1 tablespoon lime juice

1 Place ginger, soy sauce and sesame oil in a glass or ceramic bowl and mix to combine. Add tofu, turn to coat and marinate for 10 minutes. Heat a nonstick frying pan over a medium heat. Drain tofu, add to pan and cook for 2 minutes each side or until golden. Remove and set aside.

2 To make salsa, place mango, mint, chilli, sugar and lime juice in a bowl and mix to combine.

3 To assemble, top each piece of bread with spinach leaves, tomatoes, tofu and salsa. Roll up and wrap in greaseproof paper or tie with a napkin to secure.

Serves 4

Tofu Lavash with Salsa,
Vegetable Skewers with Tahini

Purple box Mosmania Red placemat RICE

BROCCOLI AND CASHEW FRITTERS

1 cup/125 g/4 oz besan (chickpea) flour
1 teaspoon garam masala
1 teaspoon ground cumin
1 teaspoon ground coriander
1 teaspoon curry powder
$^1/_2$ teaspoon baking powder
$^1/_2$ teaspoon chilli powder
1 cup/250 mL/8 fl oz water
2 tablespoons vegetable oil
125 g/4 oz cashews, chopped
4 spring onions, finely chopped
3 tablespoons chopped fresh coriander
vegetable oil for deep-frying
1 kg/2 lb broccoli florets

MANGO MINT CHUTNEY
1 onion, chopped
3 fresh green chillies, chopped
1 bunch fresh mint
1 tablespoon finely grated fresh ginger
$^1/_2$ cup/155 g/5 oz mango chutney
2 tablespoons lemon juice

Besan (chickpea) flour is used extensively in Indian cooking and is available from Oriental food stores and some supermarkets. Alternatively, you can make your own by lightly roasting uncooked chickpeas, then using a food processor or blender, grind them to make a flour.

1   Sift flour, garam masala, cumin, ground coriander and curry, baking and chilli powders together into a bowl. Stir in water and oil and mix to make a smooth batter. Add cashews, spring onions and fresh coriander and mix to combine.

2   Heat oil in a large saucepan over a high heat until a cube of bread dropped in browns in 50 seconds. Dip broccoli into batter and deep-fry, in batches, for 3-5 minutes or until golden. Drain on absorbent kitchen paper.

3   To make chutney, place onion, chillies, mint leaves, ginger, chutney and lemon juice in a food processor and process to combine. Serve with fritters.

Serves 6

16

TOMATO AND RICOTTA PANINI

6 plum (egg or Italian) tomatoes,
halved lengthwise
olive oil
315 g/10 oz ricotta cheese, drained
2 tablespoons chopped fresh basil
2 teaspoons crushed black peppercorns
1 tablespoon hot chilli sauce
4 Turkish (pide) bread rounds, split
125 g/4 oz baby spinach leaves

1   Place tomatoes, cut side up, on a
baking tray, sprinkle with a little oil and
bake for 35 minutes or until soft.

2   Place ricotta cheese, basil, black
peppercorns and chilli sauce in a bowl
and mix to combine. Spread ricotta
mixture over the bases of the bread
rounds, then top with roasted tomatoes
and spinach leaves and cover with bread
tops. Brush sandwiches with oil, place
in a preheated frying pan and cook over
a low heat for 2-3 minutes each side or
until golden and warmed through.

Serves 4

*Above: Tomato and Ricotta Panini
Opposite: Broccoli and Cashew
Fritters*

Oven temperature
200°C, 400°F, Gas 6

Turkish bread (pide) is a flat
white leavened bread
similar to Italian flatbread.
It is usually baked in ovals
measuring 30-40 cm/12-16 in
or sometimes as 10 cm/4 in
rounds. If Turkish bread
(pide) is unavailable,
country-style Italian bread,
rye bread, sour dough,
ciabatta or focaccia could
be used instead.

Breads, Pancakes &...

*Previous pages: South of the
Border Pizzetta, Red Hot Tomato
Cases*
Striped rug Mosmania *Silver wooden tray*
Corso de Fiori

RED HOT TOMATO CASES

Oven temperature
180°C, 350°F, Gas 4

Bocconcini are small balls
of fresh mozzarella cheese.
It is available from cheese
shops and some
supermarkets. Ordinary
fresh mozzarella could be
used instead for this recipe,
simply cut it into pieces
about 2.5 cm/1 in square.

1 loaf unsliced white bread
olive oil
1 tablespoon balsamic vinegar
freshly ground black pepper
200 g/6^{1}/$_{2}$ oz bocconcini cheese, sliced
4 plum (egg or Italian) tomatoes,
chopped
1 red onion, thinly sliced
2 cloves garlic, crushed
2 fresh red chillies, finely chopped
1 tablespoon capers, drained
1 tablespoon shredded fresh basil

Serves 4

1 Using a serrated edged knife cut
crusts from bread, then cut bread into
4 thick slices – each slice should be
about 7.5 cm/3 in thick. Remove centre
from each bread slice to make bread
cases with 1 cm/^{1}/$_{2}$ in borders. Brush
with oil, place on a baking tray and
bake for 15 minutes or until golden.

2 Place vinegar, 2 tablespoons olive
oil and black pepper to taste in
a bowl and whisk to combine. Add
bocconcini, tomatoes, onion, garlic,
chillies, capers and basil and toss to
combine. Spoon mixture into bread
cases and serve immediately.

CHILLI AND CHEESE QUESADILLAS

The poblano chilli is a mild
chilli and is one of the most
popular chillies used in
Mexico. If poblano chillies
are unavailable one of the
other mild chilli varieties
such as pimento, Anaheim
or New Mexico could be
used instead. For more
information about chillies
see page 78.

2 poblano chillies
4 flour tortillas
315 g/10 oz vintage Cheddar cheese,
grated
2 spring onions, sliced
90 g/3 oz sun-dried tomatoes,
finely chopped
olive oil spray

CREAMY BUTTERMILK DRESSING
^{1}/$_{2}$ cup/125 mL/4 fl oz cream (double)
2 tablespoons buttermilk

1 Char-grill chillies on a rack over an
open flame or under a hot grill until
skins blacken. Transfer chillies to a
bowl, cover with plastic food wrap and
set aside until cool enough to handle.
Using a small sharp knife, scrape away
blackened skin. Do not rinse the
chillies as much of the flavour will be
lost. Cut chillies in half, remove seeds
and cut flesh into thin strips.

2 To make dressing, combine cream
and milk in a bowl. Set aside.

3 Heat a large nonstick frying pan over
a medium heat and cook tortillas, one
at a time, for 10 seconds each side.

4 Place tortillas on work surface and
sprinkle one-half of each with one-
quarter of the cheese, leaving 1 cm/
^{1}/$_{2}$ in border. Then top each with one-
quarter each of the roasted chillies strips,
spring onions and sun-dried tomatoes.
Fold tortillas over to enclose filling.

5 Lightly spray tortillas with oil spray.
Then place, two at a time, in a large
nonstick frying pan over a medium
heat, weight with a plate and cook for
2 minutes or until bottom is crisp and
golden. Turn over, weight again and
cook for 2-3 minutes longer or until
crisp and golden. To serve, cut into
pieces and accompany with dressing.

Serves 4

Pewter plate, red and biege fabric Camargue

SOUTH OF THE BORDER PIZZETTA

Chilli and Cheese Quesadillas

4 x 15 cm/6 in purchased small
pizza bases
1 cup/250 mL/8 fl oz bottled hot
tomato salsa
440 g/14 oz canned red kidney beans,
rinsed and drained
1 red pepper, sliced
4 spring onions, sliced
2 pickled jalapeño chillies,
thinly sliced
2 tablespoons chopped fresh basil
60 g/2 oz grated mozzarella cheese
30 g/1 oz grated tasty cheese
(mature Cheddar)
$^1/_2$ cup/125 g/4 oz sour cream
125 g/4 oz corn chips

1   Spread pizza bases with salsa. Then
top with beans, red pepper, spring
onions, chillies and basil. Sprinkle with
mozzarella and tasty (mature Cheddar)
cheeses.

2   Bake for 15 minutes or until base
is crisp, cheese melts and is golden.
Serve topped with sour cream and corn
chips.

Serves 4

Oven temperature
200°C, 400°F, Gas 6

Pickled jalapeño chillies are
available in cans or bottles
from specialty food stores.
For more information about
chillies see page 78.

21

Mexican Bean Pancakes

2 cups/250g/8 oz self-raising flour
1/4 teaspoon cayenne pepper
2 cups/500 mL/16 fl oz buttermilk
2 eggs, lightly beaten
60 g/2 oz butter, melted
315 g/10 oz canned red kidney beans, rinsed and drained
250 g/8 oz sour cream
200 g/6 1/2 oz bottled hot tomato salsa

GUACAMOLE
1 large avocado, roughly chopped
2 tablespoons sour cream
2 teaspoons lemon juice
1 teaspoon chilli sauce

1 Place flour, cayenne pepper, buttermilk, eggs and butter in a food processor and process for 10 seconds or until smooth. Transfer mixture to a bowl, add beans and mix to combine.

2 Pour 1/4 cup/60 mL/2 fl oz batter in a lightly greased 18 cm/7 in crêpe or frying pan and tilt pan so batter covers base evenly. Cook over a high heat for 1-2 minutes or until lightly brown. Turn pancake over and cook on second side for 1 minute. Set aside and keep warm. Repeat with remaining batter to make 12 pancakes.

3 To make guacamole, place avocado, sour cream, lemon juice and chilli sauce in a bowl and mix to combine.

4 To serve, stack pancakes onto serving plates, then top with a spoonful each of guacamole, sour cream and salsa.

Serves 4

Mexican Bean Pancakes

22

SPICY PANCAKES WITH BEET SALAD

90 g/3 oz feta cheese, crumbled

SPICY PANCAKES
1/2 cup/60 g/2 oz self-raising flour
1/2 cup/75 g/2 1/2 oz wholemeal flour
1/2 teaspoon ground cumin
1/2 teaspoon ground coriander
1/2 teaspoon ground cinnamon
1/4 teaspoon ground cardamom
2 teaspoons finely grated orange rind
1 cup/250 mL/8 fl oz milk
2 eggs, lightly beaten

BEET SALAD
6 baby beetroot, scrubbed and
tops trimmed
1 red onion, cut into thin wedges
1 teaspoon sugar
2 tablespoons balsamic vinegar
2 tablespoons chopped fresh dill

1   To make salad, boil or microwave beetroot until tender. Drain and set aside until cool enough to handle. Remove skins from beetroot and cut into thin wedges. Place beetroot, onion, sugar and vinegar in a bowl and toss to combine. Cover and refrigerate until ready to serve. Just prior to serving, add dill and toss to combine.

2   To make pancakes, sift self-raising and wholemeal flours, cumin, coriander, cinnamon and cardamom together into a bowl. Return husks to bowl and make a well in the centre. Combine orange rind, milk and eggs, pour into well in dry ingredients and whisk until mixture is smooth. Cover and stand for 20 minutes.

3   Pour 2 tablespoons batter in a lightly greased 18 cm/7 in crêpe or frying pan and tilt pan so batter covers base evenly. Cook over a high heat for 1-2 minutes or until lightly brown. Turn pancake over and cook on second side for 1 minute. Remove pancake from pan, set aside and keep warm. Repeat with remaining batter to make 12 pancakes.

4   To serve, fold pancakes into quarters, place on serving plates, accompany with beetroot salad and scatter with cheese.

Serves 4

When preparing beetroot for cooking leave about 5 cm/2 in of the stalk attached. Wash beetroot to remove any dirt, but take care not to break the skin. This will prevent the beetroot from bleeding and help to retain its wonderful rich colour.

Spicy Pancakes with Beet Salad

Coloured bowls RICE Soup plate, teatowel Camargue

Above: Thyme and Chilli Corn Bread
Opposite: Blue Cheese Scrolls

THYME AND CHILLI CORN BREAD

Oven temperature
190°C, 375°F, Gas 5

1 cup/155 g/5 oz wholemeal flour
³/4 cup/125 g/4 oz corn meal (polenta)
3 teaspoons baking powder
60 g/2 oz grated Parmesan cheese
2 tablespoons chopped fresh thyme
1 teaspoon finely grated lemon rind
¹/2 teaspoon chilli flakes
155 mL/5 fl oz milk
¹/4 cup/60 mL/2 fl oz olive oil
2 eggs, lightly beaten
3 sprigs fresh thyme

1 Sift flour, corn meal (polenta) and baking powder together into a bowl. Return husks to bowl. Add Parmesan cheese, thyme, lemon rind and chilli flakes and mix to combine.

2 Place milk, oil and eggs in a bowl and whisk to combine. Stir milk mixture into dry ingredients and mix well.

3 Spoon mixture into a lightly greased 11 x 21 cm/4¹/2 x 8¹/2 in loaf tin. Smooth surface of batter with a knife, decorate with thyme sprigs and bake for 45 minutes or until loaf is cooked when tested with a skewer. Stand loaf in tin for 5 minutes before turning onto a wire rack to cool slightly. Serve warm.

Lemon thyme is a delicious alternative to ordinary thyme in this recipe. If using lemon thyme omit the lemon rind.

Makes an 11 x 21 cm/4¹/2 x 8¹/2 in loaf

BLUE CHEESE SCROLLS

3 cups/375 g/12 oz flour
2¹/₂ teaspoons baking powder
2 teaspoons ground cumin
pinch salt
90 g/30 oz butter, chopped into
small pieces
³/₄ cup/185 mL/6 fl oz buttermilk

CHEESE AND CHIVES FILLING
155 g/5 oz soft blue cheese
4 tablespoons snipped fresh chives
1 egg yolk
crushed black peppercorns

1 Sift flour, baking powder, cumin and salt together into a bowl. Rub butter into flour mixture with fingertips until mixture resembles fine breadcrumbs.

2 Stir in milk and mix to form a soft dough. Turn dough onto a lightly floured surface and knead lightly. Press out dough to make a 2 cm/³/₄ in thick rectangle.

3 To make filling, place cheese, chives, egg yolk and black pepper to taste in a bowl and mix to make a smooth paste. Spread filling evenly over dough leaving a 2 cm/³/₄ in border. With one long side facing you, fold one-third of the dough into the centre, then fold the remaining one-third over the top to cover. Cut into 2 cm/³/₄ in thick slices. Place on a greased and floured baking tray and bake for 15 minutes or until scrolls are puffed and golden.

Makes 12

Oven temperature
200°C, 400°F, Gas 6

Buttermilk used to be the product left after butter making. However today it is commercially produced by adding a special bacteria to low-fat milk. Buttermilk has a thick texture with a tangy flavour. It is readily available from most larger supermarkets.

Pewter mustard bowl and spoon Mosmania Napkin Corso de Fiori

PATTIES WITH ROCKET TABBOULEH

1 cup/185 g/6 oz burghul
(cracked wheat)
1¹/₂ cups/375 mL/12 fl oz warm water
185 g/6 oz cherry tomatoes, halved
125 g/4 oz rocket leaves
4 tablespoons fresh mint leaves
2 tablespoons lemon juice
1 tablespoon olive oil
freshly ground black pepper

CHICKPEA PATTIES
500 g/1 lb canned chickpeas, rinsed
and drained
155 g/5 oz soft goat's cheese, crumbled
1¹/₂ cups/90 g/3 oz breadcrumbs,
made from stale bread
2 tablespoons chopped fresh coriander
2 teaspoons ground cumin
2 eggs
vegetable oil for shallow-frying

1   Place burghul (cracked wheat) in a bowl, pour over warm water to cover and stand for 5 minutes or until water is absorbed. Add tomatoes, rocket, mint, lemon juice, oil and black pepper to taste and toss to combine.

2   To make patties, place chickpeas in a food processor and process to roughly chop. Transfer to a bowl, add cheese, breadcrumbs, coriander, cumin and eggs and mix well. Take 3 tablespoons of mixture and shape into patties. Heat oil in a frying pan over a medium heat and shallow-fry patties for 2 minutes each side or until golden and heated through. Serve with tabbouleh.

Serves 4

For a complete meal serve with side dishes of hummus and baba ganoush.

LAYERED BREAD SALAD

1 loaf stale coarse-texture bread, such
as Italian-style country bread or
Turkish (pide) bread, cut into
large pieces
2 yellow or green peppers, roasted,
skins removed, cut into thick strips
2 red peppers, roasted, skins removed,
cut into thick strips
185 g/6 oz semi-dried tomatoes
185 g/6 oz yellow teardrop or
cherry tomatoes
185 g/6 oz bocconcini cheese, sliced
125 g/4 oz marinated black olives
1 red onion, thinly sliced
1 bunch fresh basil
2 tablespoons capers, drained

CHILLI DRESSING
6 cloves garlic, crushed
2 fresh red chillies, finely chopped
1 cup/250 mL/8 fl oz olive oil
1 tablespoon chilli oil
4 tablespoons balsamic vinegar

1   To make dressing, combine garlic, chillies, olive and chilli oils and vinegar in a bowl. Set aside.

2   Place bread in a bowl, drizzle with just enough dressing to lightly coat it and set aside.

3   Place yellow or green and red peppers, semi-dried and teardrop or cherry tomatoes, bocconcini, olives, onion, basil leaves and capers in a bowl and toss to combine.

4   Place half the bread in a layer in the base of a large serving bowl, then top with half the vegetable mixture. Repeat layers, drizzle with remaining dressing, cover and stand at room temperature for 1 hour before serving.

Serves 6

Use a very firm textured, chewy bread for this recipe, otherwise the salad will end up a soggy mess, a peasant-style Italian bread is ideal. Bocconcini are small balls of fresh mozzarella cheese, for more information see hint on page 20.

White bowls, soup plate Camargue

Salads
& Soups

MOROCCAN VEGETABLE SALAD

Previous pages: Pasta and Asparagus Salad, Moroccan Vegetable Salad

Oven temperature
220°C, 425°F, Gas 7

Harissa is a hot chilli paste used in North African cooking. It is available from specialty food shops or you can make a simple version yourself by combining 2 tablespoons each of chilli powder, ground cumin, tomato paste (purée) and olive oil with 1 teaspoon salt.

10 baby onions, peeled
10 cloves garlic, peeled
3 carrots, cut into 5 cm/2 in lengths
1 bulb fennel, cut into wedges
4 parsnips, cut into quarters, lengthwise
500 g/1 lb sweet potatoes, cut into 2 cm/³/4 in thick rounds

SPICY LIME MARINADE
1 teaspoon ground turmeric
1 teaspoon ground cumin
1 teaspoon ground cinnamon
¹/2 teaspoon harissa
2 cloves garlic, crushed
¹/2 cup/125 mL/4 fl oz olive oil
3 tablespoons lime juice
1 tablespoon honey

HERBED YOGURT
1 cup/200 g/6¹/2 oz natural yogurt
2 tablespoons chopped fresh dill
2 tablespoons chopped fresh mint
freshly ground black pepper

1 To make marinade, place turmeric, cumin, cinnamon, harissa, garlic, oil, lime juice and honey in a glass or ceramic bowl and whisk to combine.

2 Add onions, garlic, carrots, fennel, parsnips and sweet potatoes to marinade and toss to coat. Cover and marinate in the refrigerator for 2-3 hours.

3 To make Herbed Yogurt, place yogurt, dill, mint and black pepper to taste in a bowl and mix to combine. Cover and refrigerate until required.

4 Transfer vegetables and marinade to a baking dish and bake for 1 hour or until vegetables are tender. Serve hot or warm with Herbed Yogurt.

Serves 4

PASTA AND ASPARAGUS SALAD

Chilli pasta is available from delicatessens and specialty food stores. If unavailable use ordinary pasta and add some chopped fresh chilli to the butter and rosemary mixture.

500 g/1 lb chilli linguine
250 g/8 oz asparagus, cut in half
155 g/5 oz watercress, broken into sprigs
60 g/2 oz butter
2 tablespoons chopped fresh rosemary
freshly ground black pepper
fresh Parmesan cheese shavings
lime wedges

1 Cook pasta in boiling water in a large saucepan following packet directions. Drain, rinse under cold running water, drain again and set aside.

2 Boil, steam or microwave asparagus until tender. Add asparagus and watercress to pasta and toss to combine.

3 Place butter and rosemary in a small saucepan and cook over a low heat until butter is golden. Divide pasta between serving bowls, then drizzle with rosemary-flavoured butter and top with black pepper and Parmesan cheese to taste. Serve with lime wedges.

Serves 4

SAFFRON AND GINGER SOUP

500 g/1 lb butternut pumpkin (squash),
peeled and cut into large pieces
4 tablespoons vegetable oil
30 g/1 oz butter
2 leeks, thinly sliced
2 tablespoons finely grated fresh ginger
$^1/_4$ teaspoon ground cumin
pinch ground nutmeg
4 cups/1 litre/1$^3/_4$ pt vegetable stock
$^1/_2$ cup/125 mL/4 fl oz orange juice
$^1/_2$ teaspoon saffron threads soaked in
1 tablespoon boiling water
1 bay leaf
1 cinnamon stick
1 cup/250 mL/8 fl oz cream (double)
sour cream

1   Place pumpkin (squash) on a baking tray, drizzle with half the oil and bake for 50 minutes or until very soft.

2   Heat remaining oil and butter in a saucepan over a medium heat, add leeks, ginger, cumin and nutmeg, cover and cook for 10 minutes or until leeks are very soft.

3   Add pumpkin (squash), stock, orange juice, saffron mixture, bay leaf and cinnamon stick and bring to the boil. Reduce heat and simmer for 20 minutes. Remove bay leaf and cinnamon stick. Cool slightly. Purée soup, in batches, in a food processor or blender. Return soup to a clean saucepan, stir in cream and cook, stirring, over a medium heat for 5-10 minutes or until soup is heated through. Serve topped with sour cream.

Serves 4

Oven temperature
180°C, 350°F, Gas 4

This soup can also be made using orange sweet potatoes or carrots instead of the butternut pumpkin (squash).

Saffron and Ginger Soup

Spoon Freedom

SPICY WILD RICE SALAD

2 cups/440 g/14 oz wild rice blend
(brown and wild rice mix)
2 tablespoons vegetable oil
2 onions, cut into thin wedges
1 teaspoon ground cumin
$^1/_2$ teaspoon ground cinnamon
$^1/_4$ teaspoon ground cloves
$^1/_4$ teaspoon ground ginger
2 carrots, thinly sliced
1 teaspoon honey
2 oranges, segmented
90 g/3 oz pistachios, toasted and
roughly chopped
90 g/3 oz raisins
60 g/2 oz flaked almonds, toasted
3 spring onions, sliced
3 tablespoons chopped fresh dill

If wild rice blend is unavailable use $^3/_4$ cup/ 170 g/5$^1/_2$ oz brown rice and $^1/_4$ cup/60 g/2 oz wild rice. The two varieties of rice can be cooked together.

ORANGE MUSTARD DRESSING
1 teaspoon Dijon mustard
$^1/_2$ cup/125 mL/4 fl oz olive oil
$^1/_4$ cup/60 mL/2 fl oz orange juice
1 tablespoon red wine vinegar

1   Cook rice in boiling water following packet directions or until tender. Drain well and set aside to cool.

2   Heat oil in a nonstick frying pan over a medium heat, add onions, cumin, cinnamon, cloves and ginger and cook, stirring, for 10 minutes or until onions are soft and slightly caramelised. Add carrots and cook until tender. Stir in honey, then remove from heat and cool slightly.

3   Place rice, carrot mixture, oranges, pistachios, raisins, almonds, spring onions and dill in a bowl and toss to combine.

4   To make dressing, place mustard, oil, orange juice and vinegar in a bowl and whisk to combine. Pour dressing over salad and toss.

Serves 4

Spicy Wild Rice Salad

TOFU VEGETABLE LAKSA

2 tablespoons peanut (groundnut) oil
6 kaffir lime leaves, finely shredded
1 tablespoon palm or brown sugar
2 cups/500 mL/16 fl oz vegetable stock
2 cups/500 mL/16 fl oz coconut cream
250 g/8 oz firm tofu, cut into
1 cm/$^{1}/_{2}$ in thick slices
1 bunch/500 g/1 lb baby bok choy
(Chinese greens), leaves separated
90 g/3 oz fresh or canned baby
sweet corn, halved
1 red pepper, sliced
250 g/8 oz fresh egg or rice noodles,
soaked in boiling water
for 2 minutes
60 g/2 oz bean sprouts
3 tablespoons fresh coriander leaves

SPICE PASTE
4 small fresh red chillies, chopped
5 spring onions, finely chopped
1 tablespoon finely chopped fresh lemon
grass, or $^{1}/_{4}$ teaspoon dried lemon
grass, soaked in hot water until soft
1 tablespoon grated fresh ginger
1 tablespoon finely grated fresh or
bottled galangal (optional)
1 teaspoon ground turmeric
1 teaspoon peanut (groundnut) oil

1 To make paste, place chillies, spring onions, lemon grass, ginger, galangal (if using), turmeric and oil in a food processor or blender and process to make smooth paste.

2 Heat the 2 tablespoons of oil in a heavy-based saucepan over a medium heat, add spice paste and cook, stirring, for 5 minutes or until fragrant.

3 Stir in lime leaves, sugar, stock and coconut cream, bring to simmering and simmer for 15-20 minutes.

4 Add tofu, bok choy (Chinese greens), sweet corn and red pepper and cook for 3 minutes or until bok choy (Chinese greens) is bright green and tofu is heated.

5 To serve, divide noodles between soup bowls, ladle over soup and garnish with bean sprouts and coriander.

Serves 4

Laksa paste and powder are available from Oriental food stores and some supermarkets and may be used in place of the spice paste in this recipe.

Tofu Vegetable Laksa

OUT OF THE FIRE SALAD

Oven temperature
180°C, 350°F, Gas 4

For perfect hard-boiled eggs, tightly pack the eggs into a saucepan, pointed end down, cover with cold water and bring to the boil. Boil for 10 minutes. Drain eggs and cool under cold running water. This method for boiling eggs ensures that there is no dark ring around the yolk and that it is centred.

12 plum (egg or Italian) tomatoes, halved
1 bulb garlic, divided into cloves and left unpeeled
1-2 tablespoons chilli oil
sea salt
freshly ground black pepper
440 g/14 oz canned chickpeas, rinsed and drained
185 g/6 oz marinated artichokes, quartered
125 g/4 oz marinated black olives
1 red onion, sliced
3 tablespoons shredded fresh basil
1 bunch rocket
125 g/4 oz fresh Parmesan cheese, shaved
6 hard-boiled eggs, halved
2 tablespoons balsamic vinegar
2 tablespoons extra virgin olive oil

1   Place tomatoes, cut side up, and garlic on a baking tray. Brush tomatoes with chilli oil and sprinkle with salt and black pepper to taste. Bake for 45-50 minutes or until the tomatoes are deep red in colour and semi-dried – take care not to overcook or they will loose their moisture. Set aside until garlic is cool enough to handle, then peel.

2   Place tomatoes, garlic, chickpeas, artichokes, olives, onion and basil in a bowl and toss gently to combine.

3   Combine rocket and Parmesan cheese and arrange on a serving platter, top with tomato mixture and hard-boiled eggs. Combine vinegar and olive oil and drizzle over salad.

Serves 4 as a main meal or 6 as a light meal

SWEET CHILLI POTATO SALAD

Oven temperature
200°C, 400°F, Gas 6

Sweet chilli sauce is available from Oriental food shops and most supermarkets or you can make your own using the recipe on page 74.

1.5 kg/3 lb baby new potatoes
3 tablespoons olive oil
$1/2$ cup/125 mL/4 fl oz sweet chilli sauce
4 spring onions, sliced
2 tablespoons finely shredded fresh mint
3 tablespoons natural yogurt
60 g/2 oz peanuts, roasted

1   Halve or quarter potatoes, depending on their size, place in a baking dish, drizzle with oil and toss to coat. Bake for 40 minutes or until crisp and golden.

2   Reduce oven temperature to 180°C/350°F/Gas 4, then pour chilli sauce over potatoes and bake for 10-15 minutes or until the chilli sauce begins to caramelise – take care that it does not burn.

3   Transfer potatoes to a bowl, add spring onions and mint and toss gently. Serve topped with yogurt and scattered with peanuts.

Serves 6

CURRIED ORIENTAL COLESLAW

¹/4 Chinese cabbage, finely shredded
¹/4 red cabbage, finely shredded
1 carrot, cut into thin strips
2 stalks celery, cut into thin strips
4 spring onions, thinly sliced
¹/2 red pepper, cut into thin strips
60 g/2 oz bean sprouts
¹/2 bunch fresh mint
¹/2 bunch fresh coriander
1 tablespoon black sesame seeds, toasted
60 g/2 oz fried egg noodles

CURRY DRESSING
1 teaspoon curry powder
1 teaspoon brown sugar
1 cup/200 g/6¹/2 oz natural yogurt
2 tablespoons sour cream
1 teaspoon lemon juice

1 Place Chinese and red cabbages in a bowl and toss to combine, then arrange in a bowl.

2 Place carrot, celery, spring onions, red pepper, bean sprouts and mint and coriander leaves in a bowl and toss to combine. Arrange vegetable mixture on top of cabbage mixture.

3 To make dressing, place curry powder, sugar, yogurt, sour cream and lemon juice in a bowl and whisk to combine. Drizzle dressing over salad, then scatter with sesame seeds and serve with fried noodles.

Serves 4

The thickness of the dressing will depend on the type of yogurt used, if it is too thick, whisk in a little water.

CHILLI NOODLE SALAD

100 g/3¹/2 oz rice vermicelli
2 carrots, cut into matchsticks
2 cucumbers, cut into matchsticks
1 red pepper, cut into matchsticks
3 spring onions, cut into thin strips
125 g/4 oz button mushrooms, quartered
30 g/1 oz bean sprouts
1 bunch fresh coriander

CHILLI AND LIME DRESSING
¹/4 cup/45 g/1¹/2 oz brown sugar
1 clove garlic, crushed
2 fresh red chillies, finely chopped
¹/2 cup/125 mL/4 fl oz lime juice
¹/4 cup/60 mL/2 fl oz fish sauce

1 To make dressing, place sugar, garlic, chillies, lime juice and fish sauce in a bowl and whisk to combine.

2 Place vermicelli in a bowl, pour over boiling water to cover and soak for 10 minutes. Drain well and place in a serving bowl.

3 Add carrots, cucumbers, red pepper, spring onions, mushrooms, bean sprouts and coriander leaves. Pour over dressing and toss to combine. Cover and refrigerate for 2 hours before serving.

Serves 4

When trying to cool your mouth down after eating chilli-flavoured foods, do not drink water or beer – while this cools the tongue it spreads the burning chilli oil around the rest of your mouth and so makes the whole experience even more fiery. A glass of milk, a cool yogurt sambal or dip, or neutral foods such as plain bread, rice, noodles or mashed potatoes are the most effective mouth coolers and neutralisers.

Curried Oriental Coleslaw, Chilli Noodle Salad

Mexican Corn and Bean Salad

MEXICAN CORN AND BEAN SALAD

375 g/12 oz canned sweet corn
kernels, drained
375 g/12 oz canned red kidney beans,
rinsed and drained
90 g/3 oz green beans, blanched and
cut into 5 cm/2 in pieces
1 large red pepper, diced
1 large green pepper, diced
3 tomatoes, chopped
2 avocados, chopped

CHILLI AND HERB DRESSING
1 red onion, chopped
3 small fresh green chillies,
finely chopped
2 cloves garlic, crushed
3 tablespoons chopped fresh coriander
2 teaspoons ground cumin
$^1/_3$ cup/90 mL/3 fl oz balsamic vinegar
$^1/_4$ cup/60 mL/2 fl oz olive oil

1   Place sweet corn, red kidney and
green beans, red and green peppers,
tomatoes and avocados in a salad bowl
and toss to combine.

2   To make dressing, place onion,
chillies, garlic, coriander, cumin,
vinegar and oil in a bowl and whisk
to combine.

3   Drizzle dressing over salad and toss
to combine. Cover and refrigerate for
1 hour before serving.

Serves 6

To blanch green beans,
bring a large saucepan of
water to the boil, add
beans and cook until they
are bright green. Remove
immediately and refresh
under cold running water.
For a delicious light meal
serve this salad on fried
tortillas or wrapped in pitta
bread.

GADO GADO

125 g/4 oz green beans, sliced lengthwise
2 carrots, cut into thick strips
2 tablespoons vegetable oil
185 g/6 oz firm tofu, cut into thick strips
1 large red pepper, cut into thick strips
2 cucumbers, cut into thick strips
12 small button mushrooms
6 hard-boiled eggs, cut into wedges

PEANUT SAUCE
1 tablespoon peanut (groundnut) oil
1 onion, finely chopped
1 fresh red chilli, finely chopped
$^{2}/_{3}$ cup/170 g/5$^{1}/_{2}$ oz peanut butter
1 tablespoon ground coriander
$^{3}/_{4}$ cup/185 mL/6 fl oz coconut cream
3 tablespoons kechap manis
2 teaspoons chilli sauce
1 teaspoon palm or brown sugar
1 tablespoon lemon juice

1   To make sauce, heat oil in a frying pan over a medium heat, add onion and chilli and cook, stirring, for 3 minutes or until onion is soft. Stir in peanut butter, coriander, coconut cream, kechap manis and chilli sauce and stirring, bring to the boil. Reduce heat and simmer for 5 minutes, then stir in sugar and lemon juice. Cool slightly. The sauce should be slightly runny, if it is too thick add a little water.

2   Boil, steam or microwave beans and carrots, separately, until they are bright green and bright orange, then rinse under cold running water and drain well.

3   Heat oil in a frying pan or wok over a high heat, add tofu and stir-fry until golden. Drain on absorbent kitchen paper and cool slightly.

4   To serve, arrange piles of beans, carrots, tofu, red pepper, cucumbers, mushrooms and eggs on a large serving platter. Serve with sauce.

Serves 6

Kechap manis is a thick sweet seasoning sauce used in Indonesian cooking. It is sometimes called Indonesian soy sauce. If unavailable a mixture of soy sauce and dark corn syrup or golden syrup can be used in its place.

Gado Gado

Silver wooden tray Corso de Fiori *Striped rug* Mosmania

LIGHTNING TOMATO SOUP

Oven temperature
200°C, 400°F, Gas 6

For a quicker version of this soup, use drained, canned lima (butter) beans instead of dried. If using, canned beans, reduce the cooking time in step 3 to 15 minutes and reduce the quantity of stock to 3 cups/750 mL/ 1¹/4 pt.
Banana chillies are a very mild yellow or red variety. If unavailable any mild chilli can be used instead. The more adventurous may like to make this soup using a more fiery chilli.

1 kg/2 lb very ripe plum (egg or Italian) tomatoes, halved
1 bulb fennel, cut into wedges
2 banana chillies
1 bulb garlic, broken into cloves and peeled
3-4 sprigs fresh thyme
5 tablespoons olive oil
1 tablespoon tomato paste (purée)
2 leeks, sliced
250 g/8 oz dried lima (butter) beans, soaked overnight and drained
1 bay leaf
4 cups/1 litre/1³/4 pt vegetable stock
2 tablespoons chopped fresh flat leaf parsley
freshly ground black pepper
125 g/4 oz feta cheese, crumbled

1 Place tomatoes, fennel, chillies, garlic, thyme sprigs, 3 tablespoons oil and tomato paste (purée) in a bowl and toss to combine. Transfer vegetable mixture to a baking dish and bake for 50 minutes or until vegetables are tender.

2 Remove seeds from chillies. Remove and discard thyme sprigs. Allow vegetable mixture to cool slightly, then purée, in batches, in a food processor.

3 Heat remaining oil in a saucepan over a low heat, add leeks, cover and cook for 10 minutes or until soft. Add beans to pan, then stir in bay leaf and stock and bring to the boil. Boil for 10 minutes, then reduce heat and simmer for 1 hour or until beans are tender.

4 Stir in vegetable purée and cook over a medium heat for 5 minutes or until soup is heat through. Stir in parsley and black pepper to taste. Serve scattered with feta cheese.

Serves 4

TOMATO AND BLACK BEAN SOUP

250 g/8 oz dried black-eyed beans, soaked for 2-5 hours and drained
2 red onions, chopped
2 cloves garlic, crushed
2 fresh red chillies, finely chopped
1 fresh green chilli, finely chopped
440 g/14 oz canned tomatoes, undrained and mashed

CORIANDER PESTO
1 bunch fresh coriander
60 g/2 oz grated Parmesan cheese
2 cloves garlic, chopped
2 tablespoons pine nuts, toasted
¹/2 cup/125 mL/4 fl oz olive oil

1 Place beans in a saucepan and pour over fresh cold water to cover. Add onions, garlic and red and green chillies, bring to boil and boil for 10 minutes. Reduce heat and simmer for 30 minutes.

2 Add tomatoes and cook for 30-45 minutes or until beans are tender.

3 To make pesto, place coriander leaves, Parmesan cheese, garlic and pine nuts in a food processor and process to combine. With machine running, gradually add oil and process until smooth. Serve with soup.

Serves 6

For more information about black-eyed beans see hint on page 10.

Stir Up a Meal

CRISPY NOODLES WITH VEGETABLES

vegetable oil for deep-frying
125 g/4 oz dried rice vermicelli
noodles, broken into small pieces
3 spring onions, sliced
2 tablespoon finely grated fresh ginger
2 cloves garlic, crushed
155 g/5 oz snow peas (mangetout)
2 carrots, sliced
125 g/4 oz deep-fried tofu, cut
into strips
1 red pepper, sliced
125 g/4 oz oyster mushrooms
1 teaspoon chopped fresh red chilli
1 tablespoon brown sugar
2 tablespoons chilli sauce
1 tablespoon lemon juice
1 large bunch fresh coriander

Deep-fried tofu can be found in the refrigerator section of Oriental food stores. Purchased deep-fried tofu should be simmered in boiling water before using, this removes the excess oil. You can make your own deep-fried tofu by cutting pressed (firm) tofu into squares then deep-frying it.

1   Heat oil in a wok until a cube of bread dropped in browns in 50 seconds, then deep-fry noodles in batches until puffed and crisp. Drain noodles on absorbent kitchen paper.

2   Drain all but 2 tablespoons of oil from wok, then add spring onions, ginger and garlic and stir-fry for 2 minutes.

3   Add snow peas (mangetout), carrots, tofu and red pepper and stir-fry for 3 minutes. Add mushrooms and stir-fry for 1 minute.

4   Stir in chilli, sugar, chilli sauce and lemon juice and bring to the boil. Remove wok from heat, add fried noodles and coriander leaves and toss to combine. Serve immediately.

Serves 4

TEMPEH AND BEAN STIR-FRY

2 eggplant (aubergines), cut into cubes
salt
vegetable oil
1 onion, cut into thin wedges
2 cloves garlic, finely chopped
2 teaspoons chilli paste (sambal oelek)
185 g/6 oz tempeh, cut into thick slices
1 red pepper, sliced
2 tablespoons salted black beans,
rinsed well, drained and lightly
mashed
1/2 cup/125 mL/4 fl oz vegetable stock
blended with 2 teaspoons cornflour
1 tablespoon snipped fresh chives

Tempeh is a soybean cake made from whole soy beans. The beans are steamed, soaked overnight, then compressed into slabs which are injected with a culture that causes fermentation. The finished product is covered with a soft white coating through which the whole beans can be seen.
For this recipe tofu could be used instead of tempeh.

1   Place eggplant (aubergines) in a colander, sprinkle with salt and set aside for 20 minutes. Rinse under cold running water and pat dry.

2   Heat 3 tablespoons oil in a wok over a high heat, add eggplant (aubergines) and stir-fry for 5 minutes or until golden. Drain on absorbent kitchen paper.

3   Heat a little more oil in wok, add onion, garlic and chilli paste (sambal oelek) and stir-fry for 3 minutes or until onion is soft. Add tempeh and red pepper and stir-fry for 2-3 minutes or until red pepper is bright red.

4   Return eggplant (aubergines) to pan, add black beans and stock mixture and cook, stirring, until sauce boils and thickens. Stir in chives.

Serves 4

STIR-FRIED SATAY VEGETABLES

500 g/1 lb fresh Chinese egg noodles
1 tablespoon peanut (groundnut) oil
1 teaspoon sesame oil
3 red or golden shallots, finely chopped
1 tablespoon finely grated fresh ginger
2 cloves garlic, chopped
2 small fresh red chillies, finely chopped
1-2 tablespoons satay sauce
1 bunch/500 g/1 lb baby bok choy (Chinese greens), leaves separated
125 g/4 oz canned baby sweet corn, drained
1 carrot, sliced
1 red pepper, sliced
$^{1}/_{2}$ cup/125 mL/4 fl oz coconut cream
$^{1}/_{2}$ cup/125 mL/4 fl oz vegetable stock
1 teaspoon soy sauce
1 teaspoon palm or brown sugar
2 tablespoons fresh coriander leaves

1 Cook noodles in boiling water in a large saucepan for 2-3 minutes or until tender. Drain, set aside and keep warm.

2 Heat peanut (groundnut) and sesame oils together in a wok over a medium heat, add shallots, ginger, garlic, chillies and satay sauce and stir-fry for 2-3 minutes or until fragrant.

3 Add bok choy (Chinese greens), sweet corn, carrot and red pepper and stir-fry over a high heat for 3 minutes. Stir in coconut cream, stock, soy sauce and sugar, bring to the boil, then reduce heat and simmer for 5 minutes or until mixture reduces and thickens slightly.

4 Add noodles and coriander and toss to combine. Cook gently for 2-3 minutes or until heated through.

Serves 4

The shallots used in this recipe are a small golden, purple or red onion used in Asian cooking. They are 2.5-5 cm/1-2 in long and have a more intense flavour than large onions. They are similar to the French échalote, which may be used if the Asian-style are unavailable.

Stir-fried Satay Vegetables

ASPARAGUS, ORANGE STIR-FRY

2 teaspoons sesame oil
2 onions, cut into wedges
1 tablespoon finely grated fresh ginger
125 g/4 oz snow peas (mangetout)
2 zucchini (courgettes), sliced
500 g/1 lb asparagus, cut into
5 cm/2 in pieces
2 oranges, flesh segmented, all white
pith removed
60 g/2 oz hazelnuts, roasted
and chopped
1 tablespoon wholegrain mustard
$^1/_2$ teaspoon ground cinnamon
2 tablespoons orange juice
1 tablespoon raspberry vinegar
1 tablespoon honey
125 g/4 oz goat's cheese
freshly ground black pepper

1   Heat oil in wok over a medium heat, add onions and ginger and stir-fry for 3 minutes or until golden. Add snow peas (mangetout), zucchini (courgettes) and asparagus and stir-fry for 3 minutes or until vegetables are tender.

2   Add oranges, hazelnuts, mustard, cinnamon, orange juice, vinegar and honey and stir-fry for 3 minutes or until heated through.

3   To serve, divide vegetable mixture between serving plates, scatter with goat's cheese and season to taste with black pepper.

Serves 4

When blood oranges are available they make an attractive alternative in this stir-fry.

QUICK RED VEGETABLE CURRY

Above: Quick Red Vegetable Curry
Opposite: Asparagus, Orange Stir-fry

2 tablespoons vegetable oil
1 onion, cut into thin wedges
1 stalk fresh lemon grass, finely chopped, or $^1/_2$ teaspoon dried lemon grass, soaked in hot water until soft
2 tablespoons Thai red curry paste
185 g/6 oz sweet potato, cut into 2.5 cm/1 in cubes
155 g/5 oz snake (yard-long) or green beans, cut into 2.5 cm/1 in pieces
2 zucchini (courgettes), sliced
125 g/4 oz canned bamboo shoots, drained
1 red pepper, chopped
4 kaffir lime leaves, finely shredded
1$^1/_2$ cups/375 mL/12 fl oz coconut cream
2 teaspoons brown sugar
1 tablespoon lime juice

1   Heat oil in a wok over a medium heat, add onion, lemon grass and curry paste and stir-fry for 3-5 minutes or until oil begins to separate from curry paste.

2   Add sweet potato and stir-fry over a high heat for 5 minutes or until soft.

3   Add beans, zucchini (courgettes), bamboo shoots, red pepper, lime leaves and coconut cream, bring to the boil, then reduce heat and simmer for 15 minutes. Add $^1/_2$ cup/125 mL/4 fl oz water if the sauce is too thick. Stir in sugar and lime juice.

Serves 4

For a complete meal, serve curry over steamed jasmine rice.

MOROCCAN VEGETABLE STIR-FRY

2 tablespoons vegetable oil
2 cloves garlic, crushed
1 tablespoon ground cumin
1 teaspoon ground turmeric
1 teaspoon garam masala
1 teaspoon black mustard seeds
$^1/_2$ teaspoon cayenne pepper
500 g/1 lb butternut pumpkin
(squash) or sweet potato, peeled and
cut into matchsticks
375 g/12 oz marinated firm tofu, cut
into 1 cm/$^1/_2$ in cubes
375 g/12 oz sugar snap or snow peas
(mangetout)
8 spring onions, sliced
4 tablespoons chopped fresh mint
$^1/_2$ cup/125 mL/4 fl oz orange juice
2 tablespoons lemon juice
2 tablespoons honey

1 Heat oil in a wok over a medium heat, add garlic, cumin, turmeric, garam masala, mustard seeds and cayenne pepper and stir-fry for 3 minutes or until fragrant.

2 Add pumpkin (squash) or sweet potato and stir-fry for 5 minutes or until pumpkin (squash) or sweet potato starts to soften.

3 Add tofu, peas, spring onions, mint, orange and lemon juices and honey, bring to the boil, then reduce heat and simmer for 7 minutes or until the pumpkin (squash) or sweet potato is tender and sauce thickens slightly.

Serves 4

Marinated tofu is available in sealed plastic packets from Oriental and health food shops. Tofu or bean curd is a good source of protein for vegetarians.

CHICKPEA AND SPINACH STIR-FRY

1 tablespoon vegetable oil
2 cloves garlic, crushed
2 fresh red chillies, finely chopped
1 tablespoon cumin seeds
1 teaspoon yellow mustard seeds
1 red onion, cut into wedges
1 green pepper, sliced
440 g/14 oz canned chickpeas, rinsed
and drained
440 g/14 oz canned tomatoes,
undrained and mashed
1 bunch/500 g/1 lb English spinach,
chopped
$^1/_4$ cup/45 g/1$^1/_2$ oz natural yogurt

1 Heat oil in a wok over a medium heat, add garlic, chillies and cumin and mustard seeds and stir-fry for 2 minutes. Add onion and green pepper and stir-fry for 3 minutes or until onions are golden.

2 Add chickpeas and tomatoes and stir-fry for 5 minutes or until heated through. Add spinach and cook for 2 minutes or until leaves wilt. Serve topped with yogurt.

Serves 4

For a delicious serving idea spoon stir-fry over steamed couscous.

Pewter star tray Corso de Fiori

*Moroccan Vegetable Stir-fry,
Chickpea and Spinach Stir-fry*

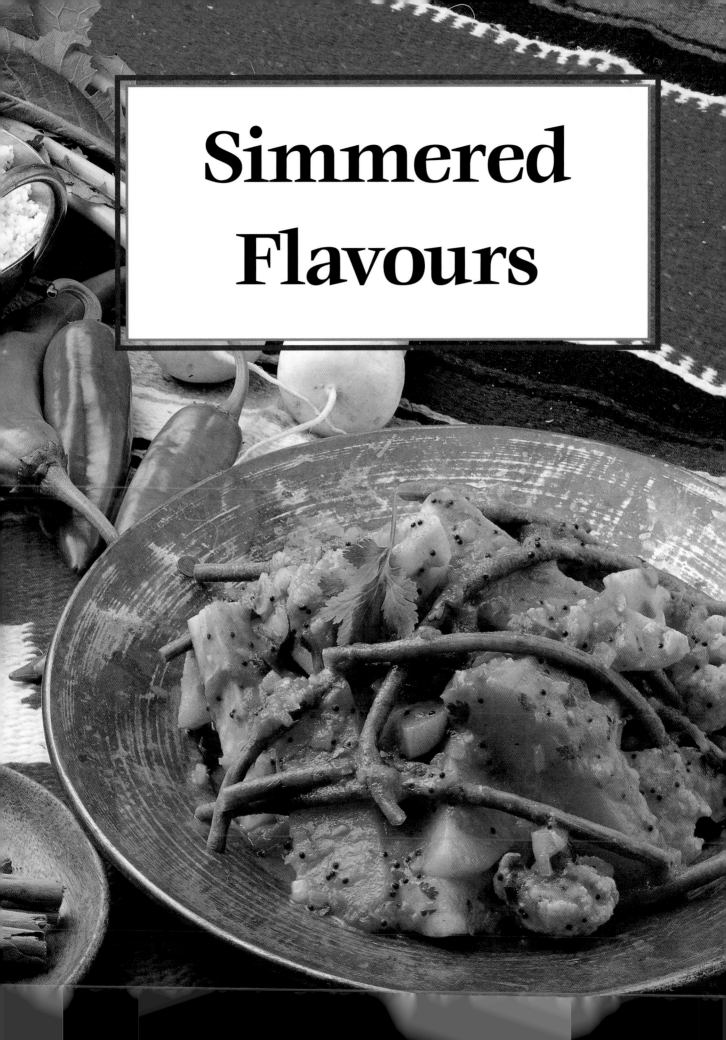

Simmered Flavours

Previous pages: Vegetable Curry with Couscous, Aromatic Vegetable Korma
Opposite: Fiery Indian Squash

VEGETABLE CURRY WITH COUSCOUS

1¹/₂ cups/280 g/9 oz couscous
1¹/₂ cups/375 mL/12 fl oz boiling water
1 tablespoon vegetable oil
3 tablespoons Thai green curry paste
6 kaffir lime leaves, shredded
1 fresh green chilli, sliced
8 small potatoes, scrubbed
8 baby turnips, trimmed
8 small onions, peeled and halved
4 slices fresh ginger
3 fresh coriander roots, chopped
2 cups/500 mL/16 fl oz vegetable stock
500 g/1 lb chopped sweet potato
8 baby eggplant (aubergines), halved lengthwise
1 cup/250 mL/8 fl oz coconut cream

Often thought of as a type of grain couscous is actually a pasta made from durum wheat, however, cook and use it in the same way as a grain. Couscous is a staple food of North African countries such as Morocco, Algeria and Tunisia.

1 Place couscous in a bowl, pour over boiling water and toss with fork, then stand for 5 minutes or until water is absorbed. Place couscous in a steamer, lined with muslin and set aside.

2 Heat oil in a saucepan over a medium heat, add curry paste, lime leaves and chilli and stir-fry, for 1 minute. Add potatoes, turnips, onions, ginger, coriander roots and stock, bring to simmering and simmer for 10 minutes. Add sweet potato, eggplant (aubergines) and coconut cream, place steamer over saucepan, cover and simmer for 15 minutes or until vegetables are tender. Serve curry with couscous.

Serves 4

AROMATIC VEGETABLE KORMA

2 tablespoons vegetable oil
1 teaspoon black mustard seeds
1 onion, chopped
1 clove garlic, crushed
1 teaspoon chilli paste (sambal oelek)
1 teaspoon ground cumin
1 teaspoon ground turmeric
¹/₂ teaspoon ground cardamom
185 g/6 oz butternut pumpkin (squash) or sweet potato, cut into large pieces
185 g/6 oz potato, cut into large pieces
250 g/8 oz cauliflower florets
1 cinnamon stick
440 g/14 oz canned tomatoes, undrained and mashed
¹/₂ cup/125 mL/4 fl oz coconut cream
125 g/4 oz snake (yard-long) or green beans, halved
1 zucchini (courgette), chopped
2 tablespoons chopped fresh coriander

For a complete meal serve korma over steamed basmati rice.

1 Heat oil in a saucepan over a medium heat, add mustard seeds and cook until they begin to pop. Add onion, garlic, chilli paste (sambal oelek), cumin, turmeric and cardamom and cook, stirring, for 5 minutes or until the onion is very soft.

2 Add pumpkin (squash) or sweet potato, potato, cauliflower, cinnamon stick, tomatoes and coconut cream, bring to the boil, then reduce heat, cover and simmer for 40 minutes or until the vegetables are tender.

3 Add beans, zucchini (courgette) and coriander and simmer, uncovered, for 10 minutes or until beans and zucchini (courgette) are tender and sauce reduces. Remove cinnamon stick before serving.

Serves 4

FIERY INDIAN SQUASH

3 tablespoons mustard or vegetable oil
1 onion, sliced
4 fresh red chillies, finely chopped
1 tablespoon finely grated fresh ginger
2 tablespoons Masaman curry paste
1 tablespoon black mustard seeds
$^1/_2$ teaspoon ground turmeric
750 g/1$^1/_2$ lb butternut pumpkin
(squash), cut into 2 cm/$^3/_4$ in cubes
2 fresh or dried curry leaves (optional)
2 cups/500 mL/16 fl oz coconut milk
1 tablespoon brown sugar

1   Heat oil in a heavy-based saucepan over a medium heat, add onion, chillies and ginger and cook, stirring, for 3 minutes or until onion is golden.

2   Stir in curry paste, mustard seeds and turmeric and cook, stirring, for 2 minutes or until fragrant. Add pumpkin (squash) and cook, stirring, for 5 minutes or until pumpkin (squash) is coated with curry mixture.

3   Add curry leaves (if using), slowly stir in coconut milk and bring to the boil. Add sugar, reduce heat and simmer, uncovered, for 1 hour or until mixture is dry and sticky. Discard curry leaves.

Serves 4

Delicious served over steamed rice or lightly spiced lentils.
Fresh or dried curry leaves are available from Indian food shops. They are the leaf of a subtropical tree native to Asia and should not be confused with the leaves of the herb called curry plant. The two have quite different flavours.

Pewter plate Camargue Wooden spoons RICE Pewter mustard bowls Mosmania

TOMATO RISOTTO CAKES

2¹/₂ cups/600 mL/1 pt vegetable stock
2 cups/500 mL/16 fl oz tomato purée
1 cup/250 mL/8 fl oz red wine
2 tablespoons olive oil
3 leeks, chopped
1 fresh green chilli, cut into thin strips
1 teaspoon caraway seeds
2 cups/440 g/14 oz arborio or
risotto rice
125 g/4 oz goat's cheese
60 g/2 oz grated Parmesan cheese
30 g/1 oz shredded fresh basil
flour
vegetable oil for shallow-frying

Serve with a salad of mixed
lettuce greens or steamed
asparagus.

1   Place stock, tomato purée and red
wine in a saucepan and bring to
simmering over a medium heat. Reduce
heat and keep warm.

2   Heat oil in a heavy-based saucepan
over a medium heat, add leeks, chilli
and caraway seeds and cook for 8 minutes
or until soft and golden. Stir in rice and
cook, stirring, for 3 minutes or until
translucent. Stir 1 cup/250 mL/8 fl oz
hot stock mixture into rice and cook
over a medium heat, stirring constantly,
until liquid is absorbed. Continue
cooking in this way until all the stock
mixture is used and rice is just tender.

3   Stir in goat's and Parmesan cheeses
and basil. Remove pan from heat and
cool slightly.

4   Take 4 tablespoons of risotto mixture
and press into patties. Roll patties in
flour to coat. Heat oil in a frying pan
over a medium heat and shallow-fry for
2-3 minutes each side or until crisp on
the outside and heated through.

Serves 4

Tomato Risotto Cakes

CHICKPEA AND ROCKET RAGOUT

250 g/8 oz dried chickpeas,
soaked overnight and drained
1 bay leaf
2 tablespoons olive oil
1 large red onion, sliced
2 cloves garlic, crushed
2 small fresh red chillies, finely
chopped
2 large carrots, sliced
1 bulb fennel, sliced
440 g/14 oz canned artichoke hearts,
drained, quartered
2 red peppers roasted, peeled and
cut into strips
440 g/14 oz canned tomatoes,
undrained and mashed
1 cup/250 mL/8 fl oz white wine
1 bunch rocket, leaves shredded
3 tablespoons chopped fresh parsley
freshly ground black pepper

1   Place chickpeas in a large saucepan
and pour over fresh cold water to cover
by about 5 cm/2 in. Add bay leaf, bring
to the boil and boil for 10 minutes.
Reduce heat and simmer for 1 hour or
until chickpeas are tender. Drain well,
rinse under cold water and drain again.
Set aside.

2   Heat oil in a deep-sided frying pan,
over a medium heat, add onion, garlic
and chillies and cook, stirring, for

3 minutes or until onions are golden.
Add carrots and fennel and cook over a
low heat for 10 minutes or until carrots
are tender.

3   Add artichokes, red peppers,
tomatoes and wine, bring to the boil,
then reduce heat and simmer for
30 minutes or until sauce thickens.

4   Stir in chickpeas, rocket, parsley
and black pepper to taste, bring to
simmering and simmer for 5 minutes
or until mixture is heated through.

Serves 4

For a speedy version of this
dish, use drained, canned
chickpeas. If using canned
chickpeas omit step 1 of
the recipe.

Chickpea and Rocket Ragoût

GRILLED PEPPER POLENTA

8 cups/2 litres/3$^1/_2$ pt water
2 cups/350 g/11 oz corn meal (polenta)
125 g/4 oz butter, chopped
1 tablespoon crushed black
peppercorns
125 g/4 oz grated Parmesan cheese
2 tablespoons olive oil
2 zucchini (courgettes), cut into strips
1 red pepper, cut into thin strips
1 eggplant (aubergine), cut into strips
125 g/4 oz rocket leaves
$^1/_2$ cup/125 g/4 oz ready-made pesto
fresh Parmesan cheese shavings

When grilling or barbecuing polenta as in this recipe it is important that the polenta is placed on the preheated surface and left alone until a crust forms. Once the crust forms completely the polenta can easily be turned. Do not be tempted to try turning it too soon or the delicious crust will be left on the grill.

1 Place water in a saucepan and bring to the boil. Reduce heat to simmering, then gradually whisk in corn meal (polenta) and cook, stirring, for 20 minutes or until mixture is thick and leaves the sides of the pan.

2 Stir in butter, black peppercorns and grated Parmesan cheese. Spread mixture evenly into a greased 18 x 28 cm/7 x 11 in shallow cake tin and refrigerate until set. Cut polenta in triangles.

3 Brush polenta and vegetables with oil, then cook under a preheated hot grill or on a barbecue grill for 3-5 minutes each side or until polenta is golden and vegetables are brown and tender.

4 To serve, top polenta triangles with rocket, grilled vegetables, pesto and Parmesan cheese shavings.

Serves 8

SOFT POLENTA WITH ROSEMARY

Oven temperature
180°C, 350°F, Gas 4

4 plum (egg or Italian) tomatoes, halved
2 bulbs fennel, trimmed and quartered
olive oil
1 tablespoon fresh rosemary leaves

BLUE CHEESE POLENTA
4 cups/1 litre/1$^3/_4$ pt hot water
1$^1/_4$ cups/220 g/7 oz corn meal (polenta)
125 g/4 oz soft blue cheese
4 tablespoons grated Parmesan cheese
30 g/1 oz butter, chopped
freshly ground black pepper

ROSEMARY BUTTER
60 g/2 oz butter, extra
1 tablespoon fresh rosemary leaves
1 clove garlic, crushed

For best results, use a wire whisk when adding the corn meal (polenta) to the boiling water. Once all the corn meal (polenta) is added stir with a wooden spoon very frequently until cooked.

1 Place tomatoes, cut side up, and fennel on a baking tray, drizzle with olive oil and scatter with rosemary. Bake for 50 minutes or until vegetables are golden and soft.

2 For the polenta, place water in a saucepan and bring to the boil. Reduce heat to simmering, then gradually, whisk in corn meal (polenta) and cook, stirring, for 20 minutes or until mixture is thick and leaves the sides of the pan. Stir in blue and Parmesan cheeses, butter and black pepper to taste. Set aside and keep warm.

3 To make Rosemary Butter, place butter, rosemary and garlic in a saucepan and cook over a medium heat for 4 minutes or until butter is golden.

4 To serve, spoon polenta onto serving plates, top with vegetables and drizzle with Rosemary Butter.

Serves 4

Round pewter plate Camargue

FRAGRANT INDIAN DHAL

For a complete meal serve with steamed rice and Indian bread.

Asafoetida powder is made from the ground resinous substance from two species of giant fennel. It is very pungent and should be used sparingly. Asafoetida is used extensively in Indian cooking and particularly in lentil dishes as it acts as an anti-flatulent.

200 g/6^1/$_2$ oz puy or brown lentils, picked over, rinsed well and drained
3 cups/750 mL/1^1/$_4$ pt water
1 tablespoon ghee (clarified butter)
1 onion, chopped
1 tablespoon brown mustard seeds
1 fresh green chilli, finely chopped
4 fresh or dried curry leaves
^{1}/$_2$ teaspoon ground turmeric
^{1}/$_2$ teaspoon ground asafoetida (optional)
1 carrot, finely chopped
90 g/3 oz green beans, chopped
3 fresh red chillies, finely chopped
1 tablespoon tamarind concentrate
1 cup/250 mL/8 fl oz hot water
1 bunch fresh coriander, leaves chopped

1 Place lentils and water in a large heavy-based saucepan and bring to the boil. Cover, leaving the lid slightly off-centre to allow steam to escape during cooking, reduce heat and simmer, stirring occasionally, for 20-25 minutes or until lentils are tender but not mushy. Remove pan from heat, do not drain and set aside.

2 Melt ghee (clarified butter) in a nonstick frying pan over a medium heat, add onion, mustard seeds, green chilli, curry leaves, turmeric and asafoetida (if using) and cook for 3 minutes or until onion is golden and mustard seeds begin to pop.

3 Stir in carrot, green beans, red chillies and tamarind and cook, stirring, for 3 minutes or until vegetables soften. Stir in hot water and cooked, undrained lentils and simmer for 10 minutes or until mixture thickens. Just prior to serving, stir in coriander.

Serves 4

Fragrant Indian Dhal

TEX-MEX CHILLI BEANS

2 tablespoons vegetable oil
2 onions, chopped
1 red pepper, finely chopped
2 fresh jalapeño chillies, finely chopped
2 cloves garlic, crushed
1 teaspoon chilli powder
2 teaspoons ground cumin
250 g/8 oz dried red kidney beans,
soaked overnight and drained
2 x 440 g/14 oz canned tomatoes,
undrained and mashed
1 cup/250 mL/8 fl oz vegetable stock
1 bay leaf
155 g/5 oz sweet corn kernels
1 tablespoon brown sugar
1 tablespoon vinegar
3 tablespoons chopped fresh coriander

1 Heat oil in a saucepan over a medium heat, add onions, red pepper, chillies, garlic, chilli powder and cumin, cover and cook for 10 minutes or until onions soften.

2 Stir in beans, tomatoes, stock and bay leaf, bring to the boil and boil for 10 minutes. Reduce heat, cover and simmer, stirring occasionally, for 1 hour. Remove lid and simmer for 30 minutes longer or until the beans are tender.

3 Stir in sweet corn, sugar and vinegar and cook for 5 minutes or until the corn is tender and sauce reduces and thickens slightly. Just prior to serving stir in coriander.

Serves 6

Jalapeño chillies are available from specialist greengrocers. They are a chilli with a medium heat rating, if unavailable use another medium chilli such as New Mexico or fresno.

Savoury
Bakes

Previous pages: Spicy Sweet Potato Quiche, Roasted Tomato Tart
Opposite: Algerian Potato Herb Terrine

ROASTED TOMATO TART

Oven temperature
160°C, 325°F, Gas 3

8 plum (egg or Italian tomatoes),
halved lengthwise
olive oil
1 tablespoon chopped fresh thyme
freshly ground black pepper
4 onions, sliced
pinch saffron threads
1 tablespoon wholegrain mustard
250 g/8 oz prepared puff pastry
125 g/4 oz rocket leaves
2 tablespoons fresh basil leaves

This easy tart can be eaten hot, warm or cold and is a scrumptious addition to any picnic. Serve with a salad of mixed salad greens, tossed with balsamic vinegar, olive oil and black pepper and topped wtih fresh Parmesan cheese shavings.

1 Place tomatoes in a baking dish and drizzle with a little oil. Scatter with thyme and season with black pepper to taste. Toss to combine and bake for 30 minutes or until tomatoes are soft.

2 Heat 1 tablespoon oil in a frying pan over a medium heat. Add onions and saffron and cook until onions are soft. Reduce heat to low and cook for 10 minutes longer or until onions are golden. Stir in mustard.

3 Roll out pastry to 3 mm/^{1}/8 in thick and cut a 15 x 25 cm/6 x 10 in rectangle. Using leftover pastry, cut 2 cm/^{3}/4 in wide strips and place around the edge of the pastry to form a border.

4 Place pastry on a baking tray, then top with rocket, onion mixture, tomatoes and basil and bake at 200°C/ 400°F/Gas 6 for 15 minutes or until pastry is puffed and golden.

Serves 4

SPICY SWEET POTATO QUICHE

Oven temperature
200°C, 400°F, Gas 6

200 g/6^1/2 oz prepared shortcrust pastry
SWEET POTATO FILLING
1 kg/2 lb sweet potatoes, peeled
and chopped
30 g/1 oz butter
1 fresh red chilli, chopped
1 tablespoon finely grated fresh ginger
2 teaspoons ground cumin
1 cup/250 g/8 oz sour cream
3 eggs, lightly beaten
2 tablespoons chopped fresh coriander
leaves

Fresh root ginger freezes well. When you want to use it, simply grate the required amount off the frozen piece. A small Oriental ginger grater is an inexpensive and worthwhile investment.

1 Roll out pastry to 3 mm/^{1}/8 in thick and use to line a greased, deep 23 cm/9 in tart tin. Chill for 30 minutes, then prick base and sides of pastry case with a fork, line with nonstick baking paper and fill with uncooked rice. Bake for 6 minutes, then remove rice and paper and bake

for 4 minutes longer or until pastry is lightly browned. Set aside to cool.

2 To make filling, boil, steam or microwave sweet potatoes until tender. Cool slightly. Melt butter in a saucepan over a medium heat, add chilli, ginger and cumin and cook for 1 minute. Set aside.

3 Place sweet potatoes, sour cream and eggs in a food processor and process until smooth. Stir in chilli mixture and coriander.

4 Pour filling into pastry case and bake at 180°C/350°F/Gas 4 for 35-40 minutes or until filling is set.

Serves 6

ALGERIAN POTATO HERB TERRINE

1 bunch/500 g/1 lb English spinach,
  blanched, drained and chopped
3 tablespoons chopped fresh sorrel
2 tablespoons chopped fresh chervil
2 tablespoons snipped fresh chives
3 cloves garlic, crushed
1 teaspoon cardamom seeds, lightly
  crushed
1 teaspoon chilli flakes
2 cups/500 g/1 lb sour cream
3 eggs, lightly beaten
30 g/1 oz butter, melted
1 tablespoon tomato purée
2 teaspoons harissa
1 kg/2 lb potatoes, peeled and cut into
  5 mm/^{1}/4 in thick slices
125 g/4 oz Gruyère cheese, grated

Serves 6

1   Place spinach, sorrel, chervil, chives, garlic, cardamom, chilli flakes, sour cream, eggs, butter, tomato purée and harissa in a bowl and mix to combine.

2   Spread 4 tablespoons of sour cream mixture over base of a 15 x 25 cm/ 6 x 10 in loaf tin, top with a layer of potatoes and sprinkle with a little of the cheese. Continue layering until all the potatoes and sour cream mixture are used. Finish with a layer of cheese.

3   Cover with foil and place into a baking dish with enough water to come halfway up the sides of the loaf tin. Bake for 1^1/4 hours, remove foil and bake for 15 minutes longer or until top is brown. Stand for 2 hours before turning out.

Oven temperature
180°C, 350°F, Gas 4

Sorrel is an old-fashioned herb that is enjoying a revival. It looks somewhat like English spinach but has a lemony flavour. Sorrel is at its best in the spring when it is most likely to be available from specialist greengrocers. For this recipe, if sorrel is unavailable use a little more spinach and add 1 tablespoon lemon juice and a little finely chopped lemon rind to the sour cream mixture. Finely chopped fresh dill or fennel could be used in place of the chervil.

BASIC PIZZA DOUGH

1 teaspoon active dry yeast
pinch sugar
²/₃ cup/170 mL/5¹/₂ fl oz warm water
2 cups/250 g/8 oz flour
¹/₂ teaspoon salt
¹/₄ cup/60 mL/2 fl oz olive oil

1   Place yeast, sugar and water in a bowl and mix to dissolve. Set aside in a warm, draught-free place for 5 minutes or until foamy.

2   Place flour and salt in a food processor and pulse once or twice to sift. With machine running, slowly pour in oil and yeast mixture and process to form a rough dough. Turn dough onto a lightly floured surface and knead for 5 minutes or until soft and shiny. Add more flour, if necessary.

3   Lightly oil a large bowl, then roll dough around in it to cover the surface with oil. Cover bowl tightly with plastic food wrap and place in a warm, draught-free place for 1¹/₂-2 hours or until dough has doubled in volume. Knock down and remove dough from bowl. Knead briefly before using as desired.

Makes 250 g/8 oz dough

BLUE CHEESE CALZONES

Oven temperature
200°C, 400°F, Gas 6

1 quantity Basic Pizza Dough
(recipe above)
olive oil

BLUE CHEESE FILLING
500 g/1 lb butternut pumpkin (squash)
or sweet potato, peeled and sliced
1 tablespoon fresh sage leaves
185 g/6 oz blue cheese
125 g/4 oz cream cheese, softened
1 teaspoon grated fresh nutmeg
freshly ground black pepper

1   To make filling, place pumpkin (squash) or sweet potato on a baking tray, brush with oil, scatter with sage and bake for 20 minutes or until tender. Place blue and cream cheeses, nutmeg and black pepper to taste in bowl and mix to combine.

2   Prepare dough as described in recipe. Divide dough into four equal portions and shape each to form a 5 mm/¹/₄ in thick round with a 15 cm/6 in diameter. Spread one-quarter of the cheese mixture over one-half of each dough round, then top with pumpkin (squash) or sweet potato slices. Brush edges with water, then fold over to form a half circle. Press edges together to seal and using a fork make a decorative pattern.

3   Brush calzones with oil, place on lightly greased baking trays and bake for 20 minutes or until puffed and golden.

Calzones make a great casual meal. Serve them hot, warm or cold with a selection of salads.

Makes 4

TOMATO AND FETA CALZONES

1 quantity Basic Pizza Dough
(recipe opposite)
olive oil

TOMATO AND FETA FILLING
1 tablespoon olive oil
2 onions, chopped
2 cloves garlic, chopped
3 tomatoes, peeled and chopped
4 baby eggplant (aubergines), sliced
2 tablespoons fresh oregano leaves
$^1/_2$ cup/125 mL/4 fl oz vegetable stock
$^1/_2$ cup/125 mL/4 fl oz red wine
185 g/6 oz feta cheese, chopped

1   To make filling, heat oil in a frying pan over a medium heat, add onions and garlic and cook for 3 minutes or until onions are soft. Add tomatoes, eggplant (aubergines), oregano, stock and wine, bring to simmering and simmer for 12-15 minutes or until mixture reduces and thickens. Set aside to cool, then stir in feta cheese.

2   Prepare dough as described in recipe. Divide dough into four equal portions and shape each to form a 5 mm/$^1/_4$ in thick round with a 15 cm/6 in diameter. Place spoonfuls of filling on one-half of each dough round, brush edges with water, then fold over to form a half circle. Press edges together to seal and using a fork make a decorative pattern.

3   Brush calzones with oil, place on lightly greased baking trays and bake for 20 minutes or until puffed and golden.

Makes 4

Oven temperature
200°C, 400°F, Gas 6

A calzone is basically a pizza folded over to encase the filling. Because the filling is sealed in during baking it is much more succulent than a pizza.

BORLOTTI BEAN MOUSSAKA

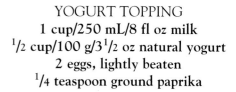

Oven temperature
200°C, 400°F, Gas 6

Borlotti beans, also known as cranberry and Roman beans, are a beige coloured bean with burgundy streaks. The dried bean is cooked and used in the same way as other dried pulses. Fresh borlotti beans are sometimes available in summer. For this recipe pinto or red kidney beans could be used instead of borlotti if you wish.

250 g/8 oz dried borlotti beans, soaked overnight and drained
2 large eggplant (aubergines), sliced
salt
olive oil
1 onion, chopped
1 clove garlic, crushed
125 g/4 oz button mushrooms, sliced
2 fresh red chillies, finely chopped
1 tablespoon chopped fresh basil
2 x 440 g/14 oz canned tomatoes, undrained and mashed
1 cup/250 mL/8 fl oz red wine
1 tablespoon tomato paste (purée)
60 g/2 oz grated Parmesan cheese
$^1/_2$ cup/30 g/1 oz breadcrumbs, made from stale bread

YOGURT TOPPING
1 cup/250 mL/8 fl oz milk
$^1/_2$ cup/100 g/3$^1/_2$ oz natural yogurt
2 eggs, lightly beaten
$^1/_4$ teaspoon ground paprika

1 Place beans in a saucepan and pour over fresh water to cover by about 5 cm/ 2 in. Bring to the boil and boil for 10 minutes, then reduce heat and simmer for 1$^1/_2$ hours or until beans are tender. Drain and set aside.

2 Place eggplant (aubergines) in a colander, sprinkle with salt and stand for 30 minutes. Rinse under cold running water, then pat dry with absorbent kitchen paper. Brush eggplant (aubergines) with oil and cook under a preheated hot grill for 3-5 minutes each side or until golden.

3 Heat 1 tablespoon oil in a saucepan over a medium heat, add onion and garlic and cook for 3 minutes. Add mushrooms and chillies and cook for 3 minutes or until mushrooms are soft. Stir in basil, tomatoes, wine and tomato paste (purée), bring to the boil, then reduce heat and simmer for 40 minutes or until sauce reduces and thickens. Combine Parmesan cheese and breadcrumbs and set aside.

4 To make topping, place milk, yogurt, eggs and paprika in a measuring jug and whisk to combine.

5 To assemble, spread cooked beans over the base of a large ovenproof dish, pour over tomato sauce and top with eggplant (aubergines). Pour over topping and stand for 10 minutes. Sprinkle with breadcrumb mixture and bake for 45-60 minutes or until mixture is bubbling and top is golden.

Serves 6

MUSHROOM AND CHILLI LASAGNE

10 sheets spinach lasagne sheets
185 g/6 oz grated Parmesan cheese

CHILLI TOMATO SAUCE
2 tablespoons olive oil
1 onion, chopped
1 red pepper, chopped
3 fresh red chillies, finely chopped
2 cloves garlic, crushed
2 x 440 g/14 oz canned tomatoes,
undrained and mashed
1/2 cup/125 mL/4 fl oz white wine
1 tablespoon balsamic vinegar
3 tablespoons chopped fresh basil

MUSHROOM AND LEEK FILLING
60 g/2 oz butter
2 tablespoons olive oil
2 leeks, sliced
2 cloves garlic, crushed
750 g/1 1/2 lb mushrooms, sliced
2 tablespoons chopped fresh thyme
freshly ground black pepper

RICOTTA AND ROCKET FILLING
750 g/1 1/2 lb ricotta cheese, drained
2 bunches rocket, leaves chopped
1 teaspoon ground nutmeg

1   To make tomato sauce, heat oil in a frying pan over a medium heat, add onion, red pepper, chillies and garlic and cook, stirring, for 5 minutes or until onion is golden. Stir in tomatoes, wine, vinegar and basil, bring to the boil, then reduce heat and simmer for 20 minutes or until sauces reduces slightly.

2   To make mushroom filling, melt butter and oil in a frying pan over a medium heat, add leeks and garlic and cook, stirring occasionally, for 5 minutes or until leeks are golden. Add mushrooms, thyme and black pepper to taste and cook for 5 minutes or until mushrooms are tender. Set aside.

3   To make ricotta filling, place ricotta cheese, rocket and nutmeg in a bowl and mix to combine.

4   To assemble lasagne, line the base of a lightly greased ovenproof dish with one-third of the lasagne sheets. Top with one-third of the mushroom filling, one-third of the tomato sauce and one-third of the ricotta filling. Repeat layers finishing with a layer of ricotta mixture. Sprinkle with Parmesan cheese and bake for 50 minutes or until lasagne sheets are tender.

Serves 8

Oven temperature
180°C, 350°F, Gas 4

Fresh Parmesan cheese is available from Continental delicatessens and some supermarkets. It is best purchased in one piece then grated as required. Once you have tried fresh Parmesan cheese you will realise that it has a much milder and better flavour than the grated powder that comes in packets.

Opposite: Borlotti Bean Moussaka
This page: Mushroom and Chilli Lasagne

SPICY VEGETABLE PIES

Oven temperature
200°C, 400°F, Gas 6

350 g/11 oz prepared shortcrust pastry
500 g/1 lb chopped sweet potatoes
$^{1}/_{2}$ cup/125 mL/4 fl oz milk
125 g/4 oz ricotta cheese, drained
315 g/10 oz chopped carrots
185 g/6 oz cauliflower, chopped
125 g/4 oz green beans, halved
1 red pepper, chopped
3 tablespoons snipped fresh chives
1 tablespoon finely grated fresh ginger
freshly ground black pepper
60 g/2 oz grated Parmesan cheese

1   Roll out pastry to 3 mm/$^{1}/_{8}$ in thick and use to line six 1 cup/250 mL/8 fl oz capacity pie dishes. Chill.

2   Boil, steam or microwave sweet potatoes until soft. Drain and place in a bowl. Add milk and mash, then stir in ricotta cheese.

3   Boil, steam or microwave carrots until soft. Drain and add to sweet potato mixture. Add cauliflower, beans, red pepper, chives, ginger and black pepper to taste and mix to combine.

4   Divide vegetable mixture between pastry cases, sprinkle with Parmesan cheese and bake for 30 minutes or until pastry is golden and filling cooked.

Serves 6

FREE FORM RATATOUILLE TART

185 g/6 oz peppered cheese, chopped

RATATOUILLE FILLING
2 red onions, cut into wedges
2 red peppers, cut into large pieces
2 green peppers, cut into large pieces
2 yellow peppers, cut into large pieces
2 large zucchini (courgettes), cut into thick slices
4 plum (egg or Italian) tomatoes, quartered
125 g/4 oz button mushrooms
3 tablespoons olive oil
1 tablespoon red wine vinegar
60 g/2 oz marinated black olives
3 tablespoons chopped fresh basil

CHEESE PASTRY
2 cups/250 g/8 oz flour
125 g/4 oz butter, chopped
60 g/2 oz grated Parmesan cheese
1 teaspoon freshly ground black pepper
$^1/_4$ cup/60 mL/2 fl oz iced water

1 To make the filling, place onions, red, green and yellow peppers, zucchini (courgettes), tomatoes and mushrooms in a baking dish. Sprinkle with oil and vinegar, toss to coat vegetables and bake for 40 minutes or until vegetables are tender. Add olives and basil and mix to combine. Set aside to cool.

2 To make pastry, place flour, butter, Parmesan cheese and black pepper in a food processor and process until mixture resembles fine breadcrumbs.

With machine running, slowly add enough water to form a soft dough. Turn dough onto a lightly floured surface and knead briefly. Wrap in plastic food wrap and refrigerate for 30 minutes.

3 Roll out pastry to generously fit a 23 cm/9 in pie dish with excess pastry overhanging sides of pie plate. Line pastry case with peppered cheese, then top with ratatouille mixture. Fold over excess pastry to enclose pie and bake for 45 minutes or until pastry is golden.

Serves 6

Oven temperature
220°C, 425°F, Gas 7

The peppered cheese used in this recipe is a cream cheese log which is coated in crushed black peppercorns. It can be found in the cheese section of most supermarkets.

Opposite: Spicy Vegetable Pies
This page: Free Form Ratatouille Tart

Something Extra

MANGO AND LIME SALSA

Previous pages: Mango and Lime Salsa, Fennel Melon Salsa, Cooling Yogurt Sambal

If fresh mangoes are not available use 440 g/14 oz canned mangoes, drained and chopped.
Palm sugar is a rich, aromatic sugar extracted from the sap of various palms. It is available from Oriental food stores.

2 mangoes, chopped
1 small red onion, finely chopped
6 kaffir lime leaves, shredded
3 fresh red chillies, chopped
3 tablespoons palm or brown sugar
2 tablespoons fresh coriander leaves
2 tablespoons fresh mint leaves
2 tablespoons lime juice

Place mangoes, onion, lime leaves, chillies, sugar, coriander, mint and lime juice in a bowl and toss gently to combine.

Serve with grilled vegetable kebabs, on sandwiches or as a side dish with curries and spicy stir-fries.

Makes 2 cups/500 mL/16 fl oz

COOLING YOGURT SAMBAL

Serve this easy-to-make sambal with spicy dishes – the yogurt and cucumber have a cooling effect on the mouth and the mint refreshes the palate.

1 cucumber, peeled, halved
and seeded
3 tablespoons chopped fresh mint
2 teaspoons finely grated lime rind
1 cup/200 g/6^1/$_2$ oz thick natural yogurt
3 tablespoons coconut cream
1 tablespoon honey

Finely chop cucumber and place in a bowl. Add mint, lime rind, yogurt, coconut cream and honey and mix to combine. Refrigerate until required.

Makes 1^1/$_2$ cups/375 mL/12 fl oz

FENNEL MELON SALSA

1 rockmelon (cantaloupe), seeded
and chopped
1 bulb fennel, cut into thin slices
4 spring onions, chopped
2 small fresh red chillies, chopped
2 small fresh green chillies,
finely chopped
2 cloves garlic, crushed
2 tablespoons chopped fresh coriander
1 tablespoon brown sugar
finely grated rind and juice of 2 limes

Place melon, fennel, spring onions, red and green chillies, garlic, coriander, sugar and lime rind and juice in a bowl and mix to combine. Cover and refrigerate for 1 hour before serving.

Makes 4 cups

Serve as a side dish with curries and other spicy dishes.

CHILLI YOGURT CHEESE

Chilli Yogurt Cheese

1 kg/2 lb thick sheep or cow's milk
yogurt
1 tablespoon cracked black pepper
2 fresh red chillies, finely chopped
1½ tablespoons fine sea salt
4 bay leaves
3 dried red chillies, halved
olive oil

1   Line a colander with a double layer
of muslin or absorbent kitchen paper
and place over a bowl. Place yogurt,
black pepper, chillies and salt in a bowl
and mix to combine. Spoon mixture
into the colander and drain in a cool
place or the refrigerator for 12 hours.

2   Take 2 tablespoons of yogurt mixture
and roll into balls. Place balls on a
plate and refrigerate overnight to dry
slightly.

3   Tightly pack yogurt balls into a
sterilised jar. Add bay leaves and
chillies and pour over olive oil to cover.
Seal and store in the refrigerator for up
to 2 months.

Makes 24 balls

Serve as part of an antipasto
platter, in salads or as a
sandwich filling. Also
delicious as a light meal
with sliced tomatoes and
crusty bread.

SWEET CHILLI SAUCE

1^1/$_2$ cups/375 g/12 oz sugar
20 fresh red chillies, chopped
3 tablespoons finely grated ginger
3 cloves garlic, chopped
2 tablespoons cumin seeds
1 cup/250 mL/8 fl oz white vinegar
^{3}/$_4$ cup/185 mL/6 fl oz water

1   Place sugar, chillies, ginger, garlic, cumin seeds, vinegar and water in a heavy-based saucepan and cook, stirring, over a low heat until sugar dissolves. Increase heat and simmer for 20 minutes or until mixture is thick and syrupy.

2   Pour into sterilised jars and seal when cold. Store in a cool dark place and refrigerate after opening.

Makes 2 cups/500 mL/16 fl oz

Serve sweet chilli sauce as a dipping sauce or use as a sauce for stir-fries and curries or as a spread on sandwiches.
Use mild to medium chillies for this sauce.

ORIENTAL CHILLI OIL

8 dried red chillies
2 tablespoons cumin seeds
2 tablespoons coriander seeds
2 star anise
1 cinnamon stick
2 cups/500 mL/16 fl oz olive oil
4 tablespoons sesame oil

1   Place chillies, cumin and coriander seeds, star anise and cinnamon stick in a bowl of water and wash well. Dry spices with a clean teatowel, then place on a baking tray and bake for 20 minutes or until dry.

2   Place chillies, cumin and coriander seeds, star anise and cinnamon stick in a sterilised bottle, then pour over olive and sesame oils. Seal and place in a cool dark place for 10 days. Shake bottle every 2-3 days. Store oil in a cool dark place for up to 6 months.

This oil is great to use for stir-fries or mixed with vinegar or lemon juice to make a spicy salad dressing.

Makes 2^1/$_2$ cups/600 mL/1 pt

Oven temperature
120°C, 250°F, Gas ^{1}/$_2$

To sterilise bottles, wash well in hot soapy water, then rinse well in hot water and place in an oven set at the lowest possible setting for 30 minutes. Before filling check that the bottles are completely dry.

HOT TOMATO VINAIGRETTE

^{1}/$_3$ cup/90 mL/3 fl oz olive oil
3 tablespoons sun-dried tomato paste
2 tablespoons chilli sauce
1 tablespoon balsamic vinegar
1 teaspoon wholegrain mustard
2 cloves garlic, crushed
4 drops Tabasco sauce

Place oil, tomato paste, chilli sauce, vinegar, mustard, garlic and Tabasco sauce in a bowl and whisk to combine.

Delicious served with steamed green vegetables or tossed through pasta.

Makes ^{1}/$_2$ cup/125 mL/4 fl oz

If sun-dried tomato paste is unavailable, use ordinary tomato paste (purée) instead.

CHICKPEA AND APPLE CHUTNEY

2 tablespoons olive oil
2 teaspoons cumin seeds
2 red onions, sliced
2 fresh green chillies, chopped
2 apples, peeled, cored and chopped
440 g/14 oz canned chickpeas, rinsed
and drained
$^1/_3$ cup/60 g/2 oz brown sugar
45 g/1$^1/_2$ oz raisins
$^1/_2$ cup/125 mL/4 fl oz water
$^1/_2$ cup/125 mL/4 fl oz red wine vinegar

1   Heat oil in a saucepan over a medium heat, add cumin seeds and cook for 1 minute. Add onions and chillies and cook, stirring, for 3 minutes or until onions are golden.

2   Add apples and cook for 5 minutes or until golden. Stir in chickpeas, sugar, raisins, water and vinegar, cover and simmer for 15 minutes.

Makes 2 cups/500 mL/16 fl oz

CHILLI AND ONION MARMALADE

1$^1/_2$ cups/250 g/8 oz brown sugar
5 onions, sliced
6 fresh red chillies, chopped
4 cloves garlic, crushed
3 tablespoons cumin seeds
3 tablespoons yellow mustard seeds
2 x 440 g/14 oz canned tomatoes,
undrained and mashed
2$^1/_2$ cups/600 mL/1 pt malt vinegar

1   Place sugar, onions, chillies, garlic, cumin and mustard seeds, tomatoes and vinegar in heavy-based saucepan and simmer over a low heat for 1 hour or until mixture thickens.

2   Pour into hot sterilised jars and seal when cold. Store in a cool dark place for up to 6 months. Refrigerate after opening.

Makes 5 cups/1.2 litres/2 pt

This marmalade is great on sandwiches or served as a spicy side dish to almost any meal.
To sterilise jars see hint on page 74.

*Chilli and Onion Marmalade,
Chickpea and Apple Chutney*

Chillies

Chilli pepper identification is no easy matter – there are several hundred varieties, they cross-breed freely and depending on the grower and location the same variety may have a number of different names.

This brief look at chillies reveals how confusing the whole matter of identification can be. When buying chillies it is best to ask your supplier about the ones available – if you are looking for a chilli for a specific purpose, such as stuffing, discuss your requirements with your supplier and hopefully they will be able to help you. More and more suppliers are labelling chillies with not only their names, but also with a heat rating and suggested uses – this should be encouraged.

Chilli peppers belong to the genus *Capsicum* and range from species which produce fruit that have no heat at all to fruit which are extremely hot. The heat of a chilli is dependent upon the amount of capsaicin it contains. Red, green and yellow bell peppers are all part of the *Capsicum* genus, but as they do not contain capsaicin they do not have the heat of chilli peppers.

Selection, storage and handling

Selection: Choose chillies which are firm and have a smooth, shiny skin. Avoid any with dark patches or blemishes.

Storage: Store fresh chillies in the vegetable section of the refrigerator loosely wrapped in a plastic food bag. Most varieties will keep for 2-3 weeks when stored in this way.

Handling: Care should be taken when preparing chillies as burns can occur especially from the hot varieties. It is generally recommended that rubber gloves be worn to prevent burns and that you never touch your face or other sensitive parts of the body with hands that have handled chopped chillies.

The capsaicin is at its most concentrated in the seeds and white ribs of the chillies, for those who like really fiery food do not remove the seeds or ribs. If a recipe does not specify whether to seed the chilli or not – it's up to you but remember if the seeds are left in the finished dish will be hotter.

Cooling off

The best antidote to hot chilli-flavoured food are dairy products such as milk, sour cream or yogurt. The casein in these products neutralises the capsaicin in the chillies. Water and drinks such as beer are not very effective as the capsaicin, which is an oil, is not soluble in them and while they have an initial cooling effect they in fact spread the oil around the mouth and so make the whole experience more fiery.

Some popular chilli pepper varieties

ANAHEIM: Available as red and green (depending on the stage of ripeness) this mild chilli is closely related to the New Mexico, its main uses are for roasting and rellenos (stuffed chillies). This long green or red chilli measures 10-20 cm/4-8 in.
Alternative names: Green (unripe) – California green chilli, Californias, long green chilli, chilli verde; Red (mature, ripe) – long red chilli, chilli colorado.
Heat rating: Mild.

BANANA CHILLI: These are very mild yellow or red chillies – some varieties have no heat at all. If banana chillies are unavailable any very mild chilli can be used instead.
Alternative names: Banana pepper, sweet banana pepper.
Heat rating: Very mild.

BIRD'S EYE: This small red or green chilli is used extensively in Thai cooking and is the one most likely to be sold in Oriental food shops.
Alternative names: Thai chilli, Thai bird chilli, bird pepper.
Heat rating: Very hot.

CAYENNE: This chilli is well known in the form of cayenne pepper. Cayenne pepper is the ground powder of the dried red pods. Fresh green cayenne peppers are sometimes used in salsas.
Alternative names: Finger chilli, ginnie pepper, bird pepper.
Heat rating: Very hot.

CHERRY: This small red chilli is usually pickled but can be used fresh in salads. It is also sometimes available green.
Alternative names: Hot cherry pepper, Hungarian cherry pepper, bird cherry pepper, Creole cherry pepper.
Heat rating: Mild

HABANERO AND SCOTCH BONNET

The habanero chilli is closely related to the Scotch Bonnet chilli for which it is sometimes mistaken. The habanero is the hottest chilli in the world and the Scotch Bonnet is only slightly less hot. Both are small lantern-shaped chillies, the habanero is about 5 cm/2 in long and the Scotch bonnet is just a little smaller. Depending on the source habaneros are said to be 30 to 50 times hotter than jalapeños!
Heat rating: Extremely hot.

JALAPEÑO:

Available as red or green this is one of the most popular and best known chillies. Being the riper form the red jalapeño is sweeter than the green.
Heating rating: Medium to hot.

MIRASOL:

In Spanish mirasol means 'looking at the sun' and this is how the pods on this chilli grow – pointing upwards. This chilli is usually dried and is used in sauces, soups, stews and meat dishes. It is sometimes ground.
Alternative names: Elephant's trunk.
Heat rating: Hot to very hot.

MULATO:

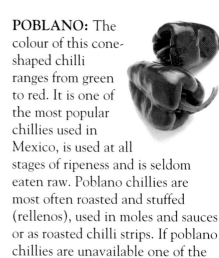

This is one of the varieties of the poblano chilli. As it ripens the pods turns dark brown. It is grown mainly for drying and is an essential ingredient for the classic Mexican sauce mole. See below for more information on poblanos.
Heat rating: Mild to medium.

NEW MEXICO:

Very closely related to the Anaheim which can be used instead of it. In the United States it is this chilli that is most often used to make Mexican-style sauces.
Alternative names: Numex, long green or red chilli (depending on stage of ripeness).
Heat rating: Mild to medium.

PETER PEPPER:

This is primarily an ornamental chilli which ranges in colour from green (unripe) to red (ripe), it has a sweet hot flavour and can be used in salsas
Heat rating: Medium to hot.

PIRI PIRI:

This is really the generic name for a group chillies that originate from Africa. The ones shown here are usually sold as piri-piri.
Alternative names: Pili-pili.
Heat rating: Hot to very hot.

POBLANO:

The colour of this cone-shaped chilli ranges from green to red. It is one of the most popular chillies used in Mexico, is used at all stages of ripeness and is seldom eaten raw. Poblano chillies are most often roasted and stuffed (rellenos), used in moles and sauces or as roasted chilli strips. If poblano chillies are unavailable one of the other mild chillies such as Anaheim or New Mexico could be used instead. The dry forms of this chilli are ancho and mulato.
Alternative names: Fresh pasilla – this name is incorrect as pasilla is the dried chiaca chilli; ancho pepper – this is also incorrect as this is the dried form.
Heat rating: Mild to medium.

SANTA FE GRANDE:

This chilli belongs to the group known as wax chillies. The pods have a bright shiny appearance looking like wax.
Alternative names: Wax, banana.
Heat rating: Medium.

SERRANO:

This green or red chilli is considered by many to be the best one for salsas. Serrano literally means 'from the mountains' and it was in the mountains of northern Puebla and Hidalgo in Mexico that this chilli was first grown.
Heat rating: Medium to hot.

Menus

Informal Winter
Lunch for Six

Saffron and Ginger Soup
(page 31)
(Make 1¹/₂ recipe quantity)

Crusty Wholemeal Bread or Rolls

Borlotti Bean Moussaka
(page 66)

Tossed Green Salad

Selection of Cheeses and Biscuits

Causal Summer
Lunch for Six

Serve this meal buffet-style in the
garden or on the patio.

Middle Eastern Garlic Dip
(page 8)

Butter Bean Dip
(page 10)
Serve dips with crusty bread and
fresh vegetable sticks for dipping.

Red Hot Tomato Cases
(page 20)
(Make 1¹/₂ recipe quantity)

Algerian Potato Herb Terrine
(page 63)

Moroccan Vegetable Salad
(page 30)

Spicy Wild Rice Salad
(page 32)

Platter Fresh Seasonal Fruit

Teenage Get
Together for Six

Red Lentil Felafel with Dip
(page 8)
Serve felafel wrapped in pita bread
as suggested in the hint which
accompanies the recipe.

Black-eyed Bean Nachos
(page 10)
(Make 1¹/₂ recipe quantity)

South of the Border Pizzetta
(page 21)
(Make 1¹/₂ recipe quantity)

Sweet Chilli Potato Salad
(page 34)

Salad of Mixed Lettuces and Herbs

Ice Cream and Fresh Fruit

Mid-Week
Dinner for Four

Quick Red Vegetable Curry
(page 47)

Steamed Jasmine Rice

Fireside Supper
for Four

Lightning Tomato Soup
(page 40)

Thyme and Chilli Corn Bread
(page 24)

Sunday Tea for Eight

Mushroom and Chilli Lasagne
(page 67)

Tossed Green Salad

Custry Wholemeal Rolls

Selection of Cheeses, Biscuits and
Dried Fruits

Index